155. 418232 MIL

KT-447-129

Alice Miller lives in Switzerland, where ~~for~~ twenty years she taught and practi~~ced psychoanal~~ysis. Now, she radically question~~s~~ ~~her earlier~~ psycho-analytic theories and psychi~~atry~~ ~~practice~~s and in 1988 resigned from the Internat~~ional~~ Psychoanalytical Association. She is the author of *The Drama of Being a Child* (Virago 1987; published in Britain in 1983 as *The Drama of the Gifted Child*), *For Your Own Good: The Roots of Violence in Child-rearing* (Virago 1987), *Thou Shalt Not Be Aware: Society's Betrayal of the Child* (1984), *Pictures of a Childhood* (1986), *The Untouched Key: Tracing Childhood Trauma in Creativity and Destructiveness* (Virago 1990), *Banished Knowledge: Facing Childhood Injuries* (Virago 1990) and *Breaking Down the Wall of Silence: To Join the Waiting Child* (Virago 1991). Alice Miller's books have been translated into fourteen languages.

In *The Drama of Being a Child* Alice Miller offers extraordinary insights into the means by which children now, and throughout history, have sup-pressed their feelings and needs in order to fulfil the desires of their parents, impeding the creativity, vitality and integrity that is authentically their own. Many people who have read her books have discov-ered within themselves for the first time in their lives the little child they once were. This may explain the unusually strong and deep reactions Alice Miller's books have evoked in so many readers of many dif-ferent countries.

ALICE MILLER

The Drama of Being a Child

and the Search for the True Self

translated by
Ruth Ward

Published by VIRAGO PRESS Limited 1987
20–23 Mandela Street, Camden Town, London NW1 0HQ

Reprinted 1988, 1989, 1990, 1991 (twice), 1992

This Virago edition offset from the
Faber and Faber 1983 edition
First published in German in 1979 as
Das Drama des begabten Kindes
by Suhrkamp Verlag, Frankfurt am Main
This English translation first published in 1981
by Basic Books Inc, New York
First published in Great Britain in 1983
by Faber and Faber Limited

A CIP catalogue record for this book is available from the British Library

Printed in Great Britain by
Cox & Wyman Ltd, Reading

Contents

Acknowledgements   vi

Vantage Point 1990   vii

New Preface   xii

Foreword   11

1   The Drama of the Gifted Child and the
Psychoanalyst's Narcissistic Disturbance   17

2   Depression and Grandiosity as Related
Forms of Narcissistic Disturbance   47

3   The Vicious Circle of Contempt   85

Appendix   142

References   146

Index   149

Acknowledgements

A version of chapter 1 appeared in the *International Journal of Psychoanalysis*, vol. 60, 1979, pp. 47ff.; a version of chapter 2 appeared in the *International Review of Psychoanalysis*, vol. 6, 1979, pp. 61ff.

As the critical apparatus of the original English translation has been retained in this edition, grateful acknowledgement is made to the American publishers of works by Herman Hesse from which extracts have been taken: Farrar, Straus and Giroux, Inc., New York, for passages from 'A Child's Heart', from *Klingsor's Last Summer*, trs. Richard and Clara Winston; and Harper and Row, Inc., New York, for passages from *Demian*, trs. Michael Roloff and Michael Lebeck.

The Winstons' translation of *Klingsor's Last Summer* is published in Britain by Jonathan Cape Ltd, London; *Demian*, translated by W. J. Strachan, is published by Peter Owen Ltd, London.

Vantage Point 1990

Almost ten years have passed since my first three books were published: *The Drama of the Gifted Child,** *For Your Own Good,* and *Thou Shalt Not Be Aware.*** Nevertheless, the facts and interconnections which I then presented, on the basis of my many years of practice, have lost neither in validity nor, unfortunately, in immediacy. On the other hand, what has radically changed is my hopeful attitude toward psychoanalysis, from which, in 1988, I officially broke away by resigning from the Swiss as well as the International Psychoanalytical Association. I was forced to take this step when I realized that psychoanalytical theory and practice obscure — i.e., render unrecognizable — the causes and consequences of child abuse by (among other things) labelling facts

*Published in Great Britain as *The Drama of Being a Child* (Ed.).
***Das Drama des begabten Kindes, Am Anfang war Erziehung,* and *Du sollst nichts merken* respectively (Translator).

as fantasies, and, furthermore, that such treatments can be dangerous, as in my own case, because they cement the confusion deriving from childhood instead of resolving it.

Ten years ago I was not yet so clear about this, my study of philosophy as well as my training in and practice of psychoanalysis having long prevented me from recognizing many facts. Only when I was prepared to end my repression, to liberate my childhood from the prison of pedagogic notions and psychoanalytical theories; when I rejected the ideology of forgetting and forgiving, allied myself with the abused child and, thanks to my therapy, learned to feel: only then did I gradually discover my hitherto concealed history.

I have described my path to this history and to my new insights in books published after 1985: *The Untouched Key* (1990), *Banished Knowledge* (1990) and *Breaking Down the Wall of Silence* (to be published in 1991). My first three books mark the beginning of this development, for it was only as I was writing them that I began systematically to explore childhoods, including my own. It was thanks to my work on those books, and later also thanks to the success of a carefully and systematically uncovering therapy, that I could see what, despite my critical attitude toward the drive theory, had remained concealed from me during the twenty years of my analytical practice.

I owe this information to my readers because I have learned from their letters to me that unfortunately some individuals, after reading my earlier books, decided to undergo psychoanalytical training or treatment, assuming that my views as expressed therein reflect the views of contemporary analysts.

This assumption is completely erroneous and misleading. The teaching structure of psychoanalysis has remained unchanged over the past ten years, and I have not met a single person who, having assimilated the insights of my books, would still be willing to describe herself or himself as a psychoanalyst. Nor in my view would this be possible, since a therapist who has gained emotional access to his or her childhood — a process that I regard as essential — cannot remain blind to the fact that it is precisely this access that psychoanalysis prevents at all costs. Whenever I am — frequently and mistakenly — described as a psychoanalyst, it is only because I do not always hear about it in time to correct such a notion.

Although, understandably enough, I feel a desire to incorporate my fresh insights in the new editions of my first three books and rework some passages, I decided against this in order not to obscure my further development. Thus I have to refer the reader to my later publications in which possible questions and apparent contradictions are dealt with and clarified in detail. There, too, the reader will find material to substantiate the statements contained in this preface.

The fight against the truth is gradually losing significance now that the new therapeutic possibilities to which I allude in my most recent books have come into existence. For each person wishing to end her or his repression, they offer access to the truth. This puts paid to psychoanalysis, even if its practitioners are not yet aware of this because they are still confined within their system of self-deception. Many of those seeking help are beginning to look more carefully at their potential 'helpers' and their views, and no longer uncritically subject themselves to psychoanalytic treatment. However, after many years of analysis it is very difficult ever to escape from the labyrinth of self-deception and self-accusation. It took me fifteen years to accomplish this liberation process – from 1973, when spontaneous painting allowed me vaguely to sense the truth, until 1988, when I was finally able to articulate it completely.

Patients and adepts at psychoanalysis, who in their circles are cut off almost hermetically from advance in knowledge, do not know, just as for years I did not know, that there is already a means of access to one's own childhood that is not (as is unfortunately very often the case) dangerous, confusing, haphazard, fragmentary, and irresponsible, but, on the contrary, comprehensive, systematic, clarifying, helpful, and committed solely to the truth. How should they know this when their teachers refuse to find out anything about it because this access to childhood fills them with fear? It is the fear of one's own history, of the truth of the naked facts that can be brought to light by this therapy. Sigmund Freud banished this fear by denying the possibility of a verifiable access to childhood reality and restricting the analyst's work to the field of the patients' fantasies.

The Swiss therapist J. Konrad Stettbacher has

described the therapy he developed, and which I tested on myself, in a work entitled *Wenn Leiden einen Sinn haben soll (If Suffering is to Have a Meaning)*. This therapy can enable many people to approach their childhood step by step and to assimilate the knowledge they had banished. With the knowledge of one's own history, susceptibility to such irrational help as ideologies, speculations, and sacrosanct lies, vanishes because blindness is no longer required as a protection from fear. Someone who has faced facts need no longer fear reality nor flee from it. This completely cuts the ground from under the power of pedagogy and of the psychoanalytical and philosophical speculations that conceal reality. It must give way to what is transparent and verifiable.

Alice Miller, 1990
Translated by Leila Vennewitz

New Preface

We live in a culture that encourages us not to take our own suffering seriously but rather to make light of it or even to laugh about it. What is more, this attitude is regarded as a virtue, and many people – of whom I used to be one – are proud of their lack of sensitivity toward their own fate and particularly toward their fate as a child. I have tried to demonstrate in my books why the disastrous belief that this attitude is a desirable one has been held so tenaciously, and to point out the tragic conditions it helps to conceal.

Again and again, readers from a number of countries have told me with great relief that after reading *The Drama of Being a Child* they felt for the first time in their life something approaching sympathy for the neglected, abused, or even battered child they had once been. They say they now have more self-respect than before and are better able to recognize their needs and feelings. 'It was *my* life you were describing in your book; how could you have known?' I am often asked.

How could I have known? Today I do not find it hard to answer this question. Today I know that it was not the books I read, it was not my teachers or my study of philosophy, nor was it my training to become a psychoanalyst that provided me with this knowledge. On the contrary, all of these together, with their mystifying conceptualization and their rejection of reality, prevented me from recognizing the truth for years. Surprisingly, it was the child in me – condemned to silence long ago, abused, exploited, and turned to stone – who finally found her feelings and along with them her speech and told me, in pain, her story. Thus, it was *my* story I was telling in *The Drama*, and many people saw their own mirrored in it.

In my fourth book, *Pictures of a Childhood*, I describe in greater detail how my encounter with this child came about once she had reappeared after long banishment and how it happened that I was able to offer her the protection she needed in order to feel her pain and speak about it. Since the book has not yet been published in England, however, I am using this preface to the new edition of my first book as a way of giving my English readers some idea of the path I have taken.

I was amazed to discover that I had been an abused child, that from the very beginning of my life I had no choice but to comply totally with the needs and feelings of my mother and to ignore my own. My discovery also showed me the power of repression, which had kept me from learning the truth all my life, and the inadequacy of psychoanalysis, which even reinforced my repression by means of its deceptive theories. For I had completed two analyses as part of my psychoanalytic training, but both analysts had been unable to question my version of the happy childhood I supposedly had enjoyed.

It was not until I started to experiment with spontaneous painting in 1973 that I first was able to gain access to the undistorted reality of my childhood. In the pictures I painted I was confronted with the terror that my mother, a brilliant pedagogue, had inflicted on me in my upbringing. I had been subjected to this terror for years because no one close to me, not even my kind and wise father, was capable of noticing or challenging this form of child abuse. Had just one person understood what was happening and come to my defence, it might have changed my entire life. That person could have helped me to recognize my mother's cruelty for what it was instead of accepting it for decades, to my great detriment, as something normal and necessary.

This part of my story – this lack of enlightened witnesses – may have been responsible for the attempts I have made in my books to provide information that would reach potential witnesses who could be of help to the suffering child. By witnesses I mean people who are not afraid to stand up for children assertively and protect them from adults' abuse of power. In our society, with its hostility toward children, such people are still hard to find, but their number is growing daily.

The spontaneous painting I began to do helped me not only to discover my personal story but also to free myself from the intellectual constraints and concepts of my upbringing and my professional training, which I now recognized to be false, deceptive, and disastrous in their impact. The more I learned to follow my impulses in a playful way with colours and forms, the weaker became my allegiance to conventions of an aesthetic or any other nature. I did not want to paint beautiful pictures; it was not even my goal to paint good pictures. All I wanted was to help the truth to break through. In this way, finally confronted with my own truth and strengthened by it, I found the courage to see with ever-growing clarity how the conventional methods of psychoanalysis block the creativity of patients as well as analysts. This is what I have tried to portray in my books for the sake of helping the victims of this process to become aware of what has been done to them and of sparing them the arduous path of my search. For doing this I have received much gratitude but have also encountered much hostility.

In the meantime I had come to understand that I was abused as a child because my parents had experienced something similar in their childhood, but had learned, as had my analysts and teachers, to regard this abuse as upbringing or treatment or training for their own good. Since they were not allowed to feel or, consequently, understand what had once been done to them, they were unable to recognize the abuse as such and passed it on to me in turn, without even the trace of a bad conscience. I realized that I could not change in the slightest my parents' and teachers' past, which had made them blind. But at the same time I felt that I could and must attempt to point out to today's young parents – and especially to future parents – the danger of misusing their power, that I must sensitize them to this danger and make it easier for them to hear the signals of the child inside them as well as of children everywhere.

This is something I can do if I help children – victims who have been condemned to silence and who have no rights – to speak; if I describe their suffering from *their* perspective and not from that of adults. For after all, it was from a child that I myself received crucial information, answers to questions which had gone unanswered throughout my study of philosophy and psychoanalysis and which did not cease to preoccupy me in the years that followed. It was thanks to the pain of the child in me that I fully grasped what so many adults must ward off all their life, and I also realized why they fail to confront their truth, preferring instead to plan self-destruction on a gigantic atomic scale, without even recognizing the absurdity of what they are doing. These are the same people who, like all of us, entered the world as innocent infants, with the primary goals of growing, living in peace, and loving – never of destroying life. I recognized the compelling logic of this absurdity after I found the missing piece of the *puzzle*: the secret of childhood, till then closely guarded. This discovery convinced me that if we are willing to open our eyes to the suffering of the child, we will soon realize that it lies within us as adults either to turn the newborn into monsters by the way we treat them or to let them grow up into feeling – and therefore responsible – human beings.

Alice Miller, Switzerland, 1986

Foreword

'If a fool throws a stone into the water,' goes an old saying, 'even a hundred sages can't bring it back.' Here we have a perfect reflection of the despair of the bright in the face of stupidity. But an ingenuous child, who still thinks in pictures, might ask: 'Isn't the world full of stones—so why should a hundred clever people try so hard to get back this one? Why don't they look around? If they do, they might find all kinds of new treasures they can't see because they are so busy searching in vain in the water!'

This may well be the case with the word 'narcissism'. The word has become part of everyday speech to such an extent, and perhaps more than any other scientific term, that it is difficult today to rescue it for scientific use. The more sincerely the psychoanalytic profession toils for a deeper understanding of the concept of 'narcissism', and to elucidate and define it for scientific use, the more the word attracts people to use it in everyday speech. The result of all this is such multiplicity of meanings that it is difficult to use the word now to define a precise psychoanalytic concept.

Now narcissism, the ambiguous noun, can be used, according to one's preference and need, to project a variety of meanings: a condition, a stage of development, a character trait, an illness. Yet, when used in its adverbial and adjectival forms, the word becomes more precise; for then it is possible to achieve some degree of complementary clarification. On top of all this, the ambiguity that characterizes the word narcissism, even in professional literature, is further complicated by the derogatory emotional overtone it receives in everyday use. For there such meanings as 'in love with oneself', 'always thinking of oneself', 'egocentric', 'incapable of object-love' have become attached to it. Even psychoanalysts are not always free of such judgemental, emotional use of the word—although they try for neutrality.

Let us now examine some of these derogatory, judgemental words. What exactly, for instance, is egoism? The fifteen-year-old schoolboy Sigmund Freud wrote in his notebook of aphorisms that the worst egoist is the person to whom the thought has never occurred that he might be one. Many people, even in old age, do not reach the wisdom of the fifteen-year-old Freud but truly believe they have no such needs of their own, simply because they are not aware of them.

Our contempt for 'egoists' begins very early in life. Children who fulfil their parents' conscious or unconscious wishes are 'good', but if they ever refuse to do so or express wishes of their own that go against those of their parents, they are called egoistic and inconsiderate. It usually does not occur to the parents that they might need and use the child to fulfil their own egoistic wishes. They often are convinced that they must teach their child how to behave because it is their duty to help him along on the road to socialization. If a child brought up this way does not wish to lose his parents' love (and what child can risk that?), he* must learn very early to share, to give, to make sacrifices, and to be willing to 'do without' and forgo gratification—long before he is capable of true sharing or of the real willingness to 'do without'.

A child who has been breast-fed for nine months and no longer wants to drink from the breast does not have to be taught to give it up. And a child who has been allowed to be egoistic, greedy and asocial long enough will develop spontaneous pleasure in sharing and giving. But a child trained in accordance with his parents' needs may never experience this pleasure, even while he gives and shares in a dutiful and exemplary way, and suffers because others are not as 'good' as he is. Adults who were so brought up will try to teach their children this same altruism as early as possible. With gifted children this is an easy task; but at what cost!

Taking a closer look, we no longer find the meaning of the word 'egoism' so clear-cut and unequivocal. It will be much the same when we examine 'respect for others', which is often said to be missing in self-centred people. If a mother respects both herself and her child from his

*Unfortunately there is no English equivalent for the word I use in the original German text, *es*, which refers of course to a female and a male infant.

very first day onward, she will never need to teach him respect for others. He will, of course, take both himself and others seriously—he couldn't do otherwise. But a mother who, as a child, was herself not taken seriously by her mother as the person she really was will crave this respect from her child as a substitute; and she will try to get it by training him to give it to her. The tragic fate that is the result of such training and such 'respect' is described in this book.

As soon as we look more closely and examine their origins, we shall see that other moralizing, derogatory words also will lose their popular clear-cut character.

The usually accepted judgemental contrast between self-love and object-love, and their portrayal as opposites, springs from naive and uncritical usage in our everyday language. Yet, a little reflection soon shows how inconceivable it is really to love others (not merely to need them), if one cannot love oneself as one really is. And how could a person do that if, from the very beginning, he has had no chance to experience his true feelings and to learn to know himself?

For the majority of sensitive people, the true self remains deeply and thoroughly hidden. But how can you love something you do not know, something that has never been loved? So it is that many a gifted person lives without any notion of his or her true self. Such people are enamoured of an idealized, conforming, false self. They will shun their hidden and lost true self, unless depression makes them aware of its loss or psychosis confronts them harshly with that true self, whom they now have to face and to whom they are

Foreword

delivered up, helplessly, as to a threatening stranger.

In the following pages I am trying to come closer to the origins of this loss of the self. While doing so, I shall not use the term 'narcissism'. However, in my clinical descriptions, I shall speak occasionally of a healthy narcissism and depict the ideal case of a person who is genuinely alive, with free access to the true self and his authentic feelings. I shall contrast this with narcissistic disorders, with the true self's 'solitary confinement' within the prison of the false self. This I see less as an illness than as a tragedy, and it is my aim in this book to break away from judgemental, isolating, and therefore discriminating terminology.

In order to avoid major misunderstandings, let me make clear that my thoughts on the genesis and treatment of narcissistic disorders in no way conflict with the concepts of drive theory.* Yet, all the work in the area of the patient's instinctual conflicts depends on the existence of an alive, true self that in the end is and

* Cf. A. Miller, *Du sollst nicht merken. Variationen über das Paradies-Thema* (Frankfurt: Suhrkamp Verlag, 1981), p. 66, which has appeared since the first printing of this book: 'When I wrote *The Drama of the Gifted Child* I still thought I could reconcile my own findings with Freud's drive theory. I considered my approach to the treatment of narcissistic disorders as preliminary work that had to be performed with many patients before "conflict neuroses" could be addressed. But the more thought I give now to the theoretical consequences of my findings and the more carefully and impartially I test the empirical content of the traditional theories, the more clearly their function in the total structure of social repression emerges for me. As a result, I have become more and more suspicious of the validity of Freudian drive theory and have experienced a growing need to distinguish between it and my own views.'
See also my book *For Your Own Good* for further remarks on this subject.

must be the subject of those instinctual drives. This is what seems to be missing in our patients. As I think back over my last twenty years' work, in the light of my present understanding, I can find no patient whose ability to experience his true feelings was not seriously impaired. Yet, without this basic ability, all our work with the patient's instinctual conflicts is illusory: we might increase his intellectual knowledge, and in some circumstances strengthen his resistance, but we shall not touch the world of his feelings.

If, however, we now take the path that was opened up by D. W. Winnicott, for instance, then the patient will reach a new sense of being really alive and regain his capacity to open up to full experience. Then he will be able to face his repressed instinctual conflicts, which are sure to manifest themselves of their own accord, and he will experience them intensely.

So when in the following three essays I try, among other things, to show my way of treating narcissistic disorders, it is not my intention to present an alternative to classical psychoanalysis. On the contrary, I am looking for a way, within the framework of psychoanalysis, by which the patient can regain his long-lost authentic sense of being truly alive.

1

The Drama of the Gifted Child and the Psychoanalyst's Narcissistic Disturbance

Experience has taught us that we have only one enduring weapon in our struggle against mental illness: the emotional discovery and emotional acceptance of the truth in the individual and unique history of our childhood. Is it possible then, with the help of psychoanalysis, to free ourselves altogether from illusions? History demonstrates that they sneak in everywhere, that every life is full of them—perhaps because the truth often would be unbearable. And yet, for many people the truth is so essential that they must pay dearly for its loss with grave illness. On the path of analysis we try, in a long process, to discover our own personal truth. This truth always causes much pain before giving us a new sphere of freedom—unless we content ourselves with already conceptualized, intellectual wisdom based on other people's painful experiences, for example that of Sigmund Freud. But then we shall remain in the sphere of illusion and self-deception.

There is one taboo that has withstood all the recent efforts at demystification: the idealization of mother love. The usual run of biographies illustrates this very clearly. In reading the biographies of famous artists, for example, one gains the impression that their lives began at puberty. Before that, we are told, they had a 'happy', 'contented', or 'untroubled' childhood, or one that was 'full of deprivation' or 'very stimulating'. But what a particular childhood really was like does not seem to interest these biographers—as if the roots of a whole life were not hidden and entwined in its childhood. I should like to illustrate this with a simple example.

Henry Moore describes in his memoirs how, as a small boy, he massaged his mother's back with an oil to soothe her rheumatism. Reading this suddenly threw light for me on Moore's sculptures: the great, reclining women with the tiny heads—I now could see in them the mother through the small boy's eyes, with the head high above, in diminishing perspective, and the back close before him and enormously enlarged. This may be irrelevant for many art critics, but for me it demonstrates how strongly a child's experiences may endure in his unconscious and what possibilities of expression they may awaken in the adult who is free to give them rein. Now, Moore's memory was not harmful and so could survive intact. But every childhood's conflictual experiences remain hidden and locked in darkness, and the key to our understanding of the life that follows is hidden away with them.

THE POOR RICH CHILD

Sometimes I ask myself whether it will ever be possible for us to grasp the extent of the loneliness and desertion to which we were exposed as children, and hence intrapsychically still are exposed as adults. Here I do not mean to speak, primarily, of cases of obvious desertion by, or separation from, the parents, though this, of course, can have traumatic results. Nor am I thinking of children who were obviously uncared for or totally neglected, and who were always aware of this or at least grew up with the knowledge that it was so.

Apart from these extreme cases, there are large numbers of people who suffer from narcissistic disorders, who often had sensitive and caring parents from whom they received much encouragement; yet, these people are suffering from severe depressions. They enter analysis in the belief, with which they grew up, that their childhood was happy and protected.

Quite often we are faced here with gifted patients who have been praised and admired for their talents and their achievements. Almost all of these analysands were toilet-trained in the first year of their infancy, and many of them, at the age of one and a half to five, had helped capably to take care of their younger siblings. According to prevailing general attitudes, these people—the pride of their parents—should have had a strong and stable sense of self-assurance. But exactly the opposite is the case. In everything they undertake they do well and often excellently; they are admired and envied; they are successful whenever they care to be—but all to no avail. Behind all this lurks depression, the feeling of emptiness and self-alienation, and a sense that their life has no meaning. These dark feelings will come to the fore as soon as the drug of grandiosity fails, as soon as they are not 'on top', not definitely the 'superstar', or whenever they suddenly get the feeling they failed to live up to some ideal image and measure they think they must adhere to. Then they are plagued by anxiety or deep feelings of guilt and shame. What are the reasons for such narcissistic disturbances in these gifted people?

In the very first interview they will let the listener know that they have had understanding parents, or at least one such, and if they ever lacked understanding, they felt that the fault lay with them and with their inability to express themselves appropriately. They recount their earliest memories without any sympathy for the child they once were, and this is the more striking since these patients not only have a pronounced introspective ability, but are also able to empathize well with other people. Their relationship to their own childhood's emotional world, however, is characterized by lack of respect, compulsion to control, manipulation, and a demand for achievement. Very often they show disdain and irony, even derision and cynicism. In general, there is a complete absence of real emotional understanding or serious appreciation of their own childhood vicissitudes, and no conception of their true needs—beyond the need for achievement. The internalization of the original drama has been so complete that the illusion of a good childhood can be maintained.

In order to lay the groundwork for a description of these patients' psychic climate, I first will formulate some basic assumptions, which will provide us with a starting point and are close to the work of D. W. Winnicott, Margaret Mahler and Heinz Kohut.

The child has a primary need to be regarded and respected as the person he really is at any given time, and as the centre—the central actor—in his own activity. In contradistinction to drive wishes, we are speaking here of a need that is narcissistic, but nevertheless legitimate, and whose fulfilment is essential for the development of a healthy self-esteem.

When we speak here of the person he really is at any given time', we mean emotions, sensations, and their expression from the first day onward. Mahler (1968) writes: 'The infant's inner sensations form the core of the self. They appear to remain the central, the crystallization point of the "feeling of self" around which a "sense of identity" will become established.' (p. 11)

In an atmosphere of respect and tolerance for his feelings, the child, in the phase of separation, will be able to give up symbiosis with the mother and accomplish the steps toward individuation and autonomy.

If they are to furnish these prerequisites for a healthy narcissism, the parents themselves ought to have grown up in such an atmosphere.

Parents who did not experience this climate as children are themselves narcissistically deprived; throughout their lives they are looking for what their own parents could not give them at the correct time—the presence of a person who is completely aware of them and takes them seriously, who admires and follows them.

This search, of course, can never succeed fully since it relates to a situation that belongs irrevocably to the past, namely to the time when the self was first being formed.

Nevertheless, a person with this unsatisfied and unconscious (because repressed) need is compelled to attempt its gratification through substitute means.

The most appropriate objects for gratification are a parent's *own children*. A newborn baby is completely dependent on his parents, and since their caring is essential for his existence, he does all he can to avoid losing them. From the very first day onward, he will muster all his resources to this end, like a small plant that turns toward the sun in order to survive. (Miller, 1971)

So far, I have stayed in the realm of more or less well-known facts. The following thoughts are derived more from observations made in the course of analyses I have conducted or supervised and also from interviews with candidates for the psychoanalytic profession. In my work with all these people, I found that every one of them has a childhood history that seems significant to me.

There was a mother* who at the core was emotion-

* By 'mother' I here understand the person closest to the child during the first years of life. This need not be the biological mother nor

ally insecure, and who depended for her narcissistic equilibrium on the child behaving, or acting, in a particular way. This mother was able to hide her insecurity from the child and from everyone else behind a hard, authoritarian, and even totalitarian façade.

This child had an amazing ability to perceive and respond intuitively, that is, unconsciously, to this need of the mother, or of both parents, for him to take on the role that had unconsciously been assigned to him.

This role secured 'love' for the child—that is, his parents' narcissistic cathexis. He could sense that he was needed and this, he felt, guaranteed him a measure of existential security.

This ability is then extended and perfected. Later, these children not only become mothers (confidantes, comforters, advisers, supporters) of their own mothers, but also take over the responsibility for their siblings and eventually develop a special sensitivity to unconscious signals manifesting the needs of others. No wonder that they often choose the psychoanalytic profession later on. Who else, without this previous history, would muster sufficient interest to spend the whole day trying to discover what is happening in the other person's unconscious? But the development and perfecting of this differentiated sensorium—which once assisted the child in surviving and now enables the adult to pursue his strange profession—also contains the roots of his narcissistic disturbance.

---

even a woman. In the course of the past twenty years, quite often the fathers have assumed this mothering function (*Mütterlichkeit*).

THE LOST WORLD OF FEELINGS

The phenomenology of narcissistic disturbance is well-known today. On the basis of my experience, I would think that its aetiology is to be found in the infant's early emotional adaptation. In any case, the child's narcissistic needs for respect, echoing, understanding, sympathy and mirroring suffer a very special fate, as a result of this early adaptation.

1.   One serious consequence of this early adaptation is the impossibility of consciously experiencing certain feelings of his own (such as jealousy, envy, anger, loneliness, impotence, anxiety) either in childhood or later in adulthood. This is all the more tragic since we are here concerned with lively people who are especially capable of differentiated feelings. This is noticeable at those times in their analyses when they describe childhood experiences that were free of conflict. Usually these concern experiences with nature, which they could enjoy without hurting the mother or making her feel insecure, without reducing her power or endangering her equilibrium. But it is remarkable how these attentive, lively and sensitive children who can, for example, remember exactly how they discovered the sunlight in bright grass at the age of four, yet at eight might be unable to 'notice anything' or to show any curiosity about the pregnant mother or, similarly, were 'not at all' jealous at the birth of a sibling. Again, at the age of two, one of them could be left alone while soldiers forced their way into the house and searched it, and she

had 'been good', suffering this quietly and without crying. They have all developed the art of not experiencing feelings, for a child can only experience his feelings when there is somebody there who accepts him fully, understands and supports him. If that is missing, if the child must risk losing the mother's love, or that of her substitute, then he cannot experience these feelings secretly 'just for himself' but fails to experience them at all. But nevertheless . . . something remains.

Throughout their later life, these people unconsciously create situations in which these rudimentary feelings may awaken but without the original connection ever becoming clear. The point of this 'play', as Jurgen Habermas (1970) called it, can only be deciphered in analysis, when the analyst joins the cast and the intense emotions experienced in the analysis are successfully related to their original situation. Freud described this in 1914 in his work 'Recollection, Repetition, and Working Through'.

Take, for an example, the feeling of being abandoned—not that of the adult, who feels lonely and therefore takes tablets or drugs, goes to the movies, visits friends, or telephones 'unnecessarily', in order to bridge the gap somehow. No, I mean the original feeling in the small infant, who had none of these chances of distraction and whose communication, verbal or preverbal, did not reach the mother. This was not the case because his mother was bad, but because she herself was narcissistically deprived, dependent on a specific echo from the child that was so essential to her, for she herself was a child in search of an object that could be available to her. However paradoxical this may seem, a child is at the mother's disposal. A child cannot run away from her as her own mother once did. A child can be so brought up that it becomes what she wants it to be. A child can be made to show respect, she can impose her own feelings on him, see herself mirrored in his love and admiration, and feel strong in his presence, but when he becomes too much she can abandon that child to a stranger. The mother can feel herself the centre of attention, for her child's eyes follow her everywhere. When a woman had to suppress and repress all these needs in relation to her own mother, they rise from the depth of her unconscious and seek gratification through her own child, however well educated and well intentioned she may be, and however much she is aware of what a child needs. The child feels this clearly and very soon forgoes the expression of his own distress. Later, when these feelings of being deserted begin to emerge in the analysis of the adult, they are accompanied by such intensity of pain and despair that it is quite clear that these people could not have survived so much pain. That would only have been possible in an empathic, attentive environment, and this they lacked. The same holds true for emotions connected with the Oedipal drama and the entire drive development of the child. All this had to be warded off. But to say that it was absent would be a denial of the empirical evidence we have gained in analysis.

Several sorts of mechanisms can be recognized in the defence against early feelings of abandonment. In addition to simple denial there is reversal ('I am breaking down under the constant responsibility because the others need me ceaselessly'), changing passive suffering into active behaviour ('I must quit women as soon as I feel that I am essential to them'), projection on to other objects, and introjection of the threat of loss of love ('I must always be good and measure up to the norm, then there is no risk; I constantly feel that the demands are too great, but I cannot change that, I must always achieve more than others'). Intellectualization is very commonly met, since it is a defence mechanism of great reliability.

All these defence mechanisms are accompanied by repression of the original situation and the emotions belonging to it, which can only come to the surface after years of analysis.

2. Accommodation to parental needs often (but not always) leads to the 'as-if personality' (Winnicott has described it as the 'false self'). This person develops in such a way that he reveals only what is expected of him, and fuses so completely with what he reveals that—until he comes to analysis—one could scarcely have guessed how much more there is to him, behind this 'masked view of himself' (Habermas, 1970). He cannot develop and differentiate his 'true self', because he is unable to live it. It remains in a 'state of noncommunication', as Winnicott has expressed it. Understandably, these patients complain of a sense of emptiness, futility, or homelessness, for the emptiness is real. A process of emptying, impoverishment and partial killing of his potential actually took place when all that was alive and spontaneous in him was cut off. In childhood these

people have often had dreams in which they experienced themselves as partly dead. I should like to give three examples.

'My younger siblings are standing on a bridge and throw a box into the river. I know that I am lying in it, dead, and yet I hear my heart beating; at this moment I always wake' (a recurrent dream). This dream combines her unconscious aggression (envy and jealousy) against the younger siblings, for whom the patient was always a caring 'mother', with 'killing' her own feelings, wishes, and demands, by means of reaction formation.

Another patient dreamed: 'I see a green meadow, on which there is a white coffin. I am afraid that my mother is in it, but I open the lid and, luckily, it is not my mother but me.' If this patient had been able as a child to express his disappointment with his mother—to experience his rage and anger–he could have stayed alive. But that would have led to the loss of his mother's love, and that, for a child, is the same as object loss and death. So he 'killed' his anger and with it a part of himself in order to preserve his self-object, the mother.

A young girl used to dream: 'I am lying on my bed. I am dead. My parents are talking and looking at me but they don't realize that I am dead.'

3. The difficulties inherent in experiencing and developing one's own emotions lead to bond permanence, which prevents individuation, in which both parties have an interest. The parents have found in their child's 'false self' the confirmation they were looking for, a substitute for their own missing structures; the child, who has been unable to build up his own

structures, is first consciously and then unconsciously (through the introject) dependent on his parents. He cannot rely on his own emotions, has not come to experience them through trial and error, has no sense of his own real needs, and is alienated from himself to the highest degree. Under these circumstances he cannot separate from his parents, and even as an adult he is still dependent on affirmation from his partner, from groups, or especially from his own children. The heirs of the parents are the introjects, from whom the 'true self' must remain concealed, and so loneliness in the parental home is later followed by isolation within the self. Narcissistic cathexis of her child by the mother does not exclude emotional devotion. On the contrary, she loves the child, as her self-object, excessively, though not in the manner that he needs, and always on the condition that he presents his 'false self'. This is no obstacle to the development of intellectual abilities, but it is one to the unfolding of an authentic emotional life.

IN SEARCH OF THE TRUE SELF

How can psychoanalysis be of help here? The harmony depicted in Käthchen von Heilbronn (Heinrich von Kleist's romantic heroine, in the drama of the same name, 1810) is probably only possible in fantasy, and particularly understandable arising from the longing of such a narcissistically tormented person as Kleist. The simplicity of Shakespeare's Falstaff—of whom Freud is reported to have said that he embodied the sadness of

29

healthy narcissism—is neither possible nor desirable for these patients. The paradise of preambivalent harmony, for which so many patients hope, is unattainable. But the experience of one's own truth, and the postambivalent knowledge of it, makes it possible to return to one's own world of feelings at an adult level—without paradise, but with the ability to mourn.

It is one of the turning points in analysis when the narcissistically disturbed patient comes to the emotional insight that all the love he has captured with so much effort and self-denial was not meant for him as he really was, that the admiration for his beauty and achievements was aimed at this beauty and these achievements, and not at the child himself. In analysis, the small and lonely child that is hidden behind his achievements wakes up and asks: 'What would have happened if I had appeared before you, bad, ugly, angry, jealous, lazy, dirty, smelly? Where would your love have been then? And I was all these things as well. Does this mean that it was not really me whom you loved, but only what I pretended to be? The well-behaved, reliable, emphatic, understanding, and convenient child, who in fact was never a child at all? What became of my childhood? Have I not been cheated out of it? I can never return to it. I can never make up for it. From the beginning I have been a little adult. My abilities—were they simply misused?'

These questions are accompanied by much grief and pain, but the result always is a new authority that is being established in the analysand (like a heritage of the mother who never existed)—a new empathy with

his own fate, born out of mourning. At this point one
patient dreamed that he killed a child thirty years ago
and no one had helped him to save it. (Thirty years
earlier, precisely in the Oedipal phase, those around
him had noticed that this child became totally reserved,
polite and good, and no longer showed any emotional
reactions.)

Now the patient does not make light of manifestations of his self any more, does not laugh or jeer at them,
even if he still unconsciously passes them over or
ignores them, in the same subtle way that his parents
dealt with the child before he had any words to express
his needs. Then fantasies of grandeur will be revived,
too, which had been deprecated, and so split off. And
now we can see their relation to the frustrated and
repressed needs for attention, respect, understanding,
for echoing and mirroring. At the centre of these
fantasies there is always a wish that the patient could
never have accepted before. For example: I am in
the centre, my parents are taking notice of me and are
ignoring their own wishes (fantasy: I am the princess
attended by my servants); my parents understand when
I try to express my feelings and do not laugh at me; my
parents are rich in talents and courage and not
dependent on my achievements; they do not need my
comfort nor my smile (they are king and queen). This
would mean for the child: I can be sad or happy
whenever anything makes me sad or happy; I don't have
to look cheerful for someone else, and I don't have to
suppress my distress or anxiety to fit other people's
needs. I can be angry and no one will die or get a

headache because of it. I can rage and smash things without losing my parents. In D. W. Winnicott's words: 'I can destroy the object and it will still survive' (1969).

Once these grandiose fantasies (often accompanied by obsessional or perverse phenomena) have been experienced and understood as the alienated form of these real and legitimate needs, the split can be overcome and integration can follow. What is the chronological course?

1. In the majority of cases, it is not difficult to point out to the patient early in his analysis the way he has dealt with his feelings and needs, and that this was a question of survival for him. It is a great relief to him that things he was accustomed to choke off can be recognized and taken seriously. The psychoanalyst can use the material the patient presents to show him how he treats his feelings with ridicule and irony, tries to persuade himself they do not exist, belittles them, and either does not become aware of them at all or only after several days when they have already passed. Gradually, the patient himself realizes how he is forced to look for distraction when he is moved, upset, or sad. (When a six-year-old's mother died, his aunt told him: 'You must be brave; don't cry; now go to your room and play nicely.') There are still many situations where he sees himself as other people see him, constantly asking himself what impression he is making, and how he ought to be reacting or what feelings he ought to have. But on the whole he feels much freer in this initial period and, thanks to the analyst as his auxiliary ego, he can be more aware of himself when his immediate

feelings are experienced within the session and taken seriously. He is very grateful for this possibility, too.

2. This will, of course, change. In addition to this first function, which will continue for a long time, the analyst must take on a second as soon as the transference neurosis has developed: that of being the transference figure. Feelings out of various periods of childhood come to the surface then. This is the most difficult stage in analysis, when there is most acting out. The patient begins to be articulate and breaks with his former compliant attitudes, but because of his early experience he cannot believe this is possible without mortal danger. The compulsion to repeat leads him to provoke situations where his fear of object loss, rejection and isolation has a basis in present reality, situations into which he drags the analyst with him (as a rejecting or demanding mother, for example), so that afterwards he can enjoy the relief of having taken the risk and been true to himself. This can begin quite harmlessly. The patient is surprised by feelings that he would rather not have recognized, but now it is too late, awareness of his own impulses has already been aroused and there is no going back. Now the analysand must (and also is allowed to!) experience himself in a way he had never before thought possible.

Whereas this patient had always despised miserliness, he suddenly catches himself reckoning up the two minutes lost to his session through a telephone call. Whereas he had previously never made demands himself and had always been tireless in fulfilling the demands of others, now he is suddenly furious that his analyst again is going on vacation. Or he is annoyed to see other people waiting outside the consulting room. What can this be? Surely not jealousy. That is an emotion he does not recognize! And yet . . . 'What are they doing here? Do others besides me come here?' He had never realized that before. At first it is mortifying to see that he is not only good, understanding, tolerant, controlled and, above all, adult, for this was always the basis of his self-respect. But another, weightier mortification is added to the first when this analysand discovers the introjects within himself, and that he has been their prisoner. For his anger, demands and avarice do not at first appear in a tamed adult form, but in the childish-archaic one in which they were repressed. The patient is horrified when he realizes that he is capable of screaming with rage in the same way that he so hated in his father, or that, only yesterday, he has checked and controlled his child, 'practically', he says, 'in my mother's clothes!' This revival of the introjects, and learning to come to terms with them, with the help of the transference, forms the major part of the analysis. What cannot be recalled is unconsciously re-enacted and thus indirectly discovered. The more he is able to admit and experience these early feelings, the stronger and more coherent the patient will feel. This in turn enables him to expose himself to emotions that well up out of his earliest childhood and to experience the helplessness and ambivalence of that period.

There is a big difference between having ambivalent feelings towards someone as an adult and, after working back through much of one's previous history,

suddenly experiencing one's self as a two-year-old who
is being fed by the maid in the kitchen and thinking in
despair: 'Why does mother go out every evening? Why
does she not take pleasure in me? What is wrong with
me that she prefers to go to other people? What can I do
to make her stay at home? Just don't cry, just don't cry.'
The child could not have thought in these words at the
time, but in the session on the couch, this man was both
an adult and a two-year-old child, and could cry bitterly.
It was not only a cathartic crying, but rather the
integration of his earlier longing for his mother, which
until now he had always denied. In the following weeks
the patient went through all the torments of his
ambivalence towards his mother, who was a successful
paediatrician. Her previously 'frozen' portrait melted
into the picture of a woman with lovable aspects but
who had not been able to give her child any continuity
in their relationship. 'I hated these beasts who were
constantly sick and always taking my mother away
from me. I hated my mother because she preferred being
with them to being with me.' In the transference,
clinging tendencies and feelings of helplessness were
mingled with long dammed-up rage against the love
object who had not been available to him. As a result,
the patient could rid himself of a perversion that had
tormented him for a long time; its point was now easy to
understand. His relationships to women lost their
marked characteristics of narcissistic cathexis, and his
compulsion first to conquer and then to desert them
disappeared completely.

At this stage in the analysis the patient experienced

his early feelings of helplessness, of anger, and of being at the mercy of the loved object in a manner that he could not previously have remembered. One can only remember what has been consciously experienced. But the emotional world of a child with a narcissistic disturbance is itself the result of a selection, which has eliminated the most important elements. These early feelings, joined with the pain of not being able to understand what is going on that is part of the earliest period of childhood, are then consciously experienced for the first time during analysis.

The true self has been in 'a state of noncommunication', as Winnicott said, because it had to be protected. The patient never needs to hide anything else so thoroughly, so deeply, and for so long a time as he has hidden his true self. Thus it is like a miracle each time to see how much individuality has survived behind such dissimulation, denial and self-alienation, and can reappear as soon as the work of mourning brings freedom from the introjects. Nevertheless, it would be wrong to understand Winnicott's words to mean that there is a fully developed true self hidden behind the false self. If that were so, there would be no narcissistic disturbance but a conscious self-protection. The important point is that the child does not know what he is hiding. A patient expressed this in the following way: 'I lived in a glass house into which my mother could look at any time. In a glass house, however, you cannot conceal anything without giving yourself away, except by hiding it under the ground. And then you cannot see it yourself either.'

An adult can only be fully aware of his feelings if he has internalized an affectionate and empathic self-object. People with narcissistic disturbances are missing out on this. Therefore they are never overtaken by unexpected emotions, and will only admit those feelings that are accepted and approved by their inner censor, which is their parents' heir. Depression and a sense of inner emptiness is the price they must pay for this control. To return to Winnicott's concept, the true self cannot communicate because it has remained unconscious, and therefore undeveloped, in its inner prison. The company of prison warders does not encourage lively development. It is only after it is liberated in analysis that the self begins to be articulate, to grow, and to develop its creativity. Where there had only been fearful emptiness or equally frightening grandiose fantasies, there now is unfolding an unexpected wealth of vitality. This is not a homecoming since this home had never before existed. It is the discovery of home.

3.   The phase of separation begins when the analysand has reliably acquired the ability to mourn and can face feelings from his childhood, without the constant need for the analyst.

THE PSYCHOANALYST'S SITUATION

It is often said that psychoanalysts suffer from a narcissistic disturbance. The purpose of my presentation so far has been to clarify the extent to which this can be confirmed, not only inductively based on experience, but also deductively from the type of talent that is needed by an analyst. His sensibility, his empathy, his intense and differentiated emotional responsiveness, and his unusually powerful 'antennae' seem to predestine him as a child to be used—if not misused—by people with intense narcissistic needs.

Of course, there is the theoretical possibility that a child who was gifted in this way could have had parents who did not need to misuse him—parents who saw him as he really was, understood him, and tolerated and respected his feelings. Such a child would develop a healthy narcissism. One could hardly expect, however: (1) that he would later take up the profession of psychoanalysis; (2) that he would cultivate and develop his sensorium for others to the same extent as those who were 'narcissistically used'; (3) that he would ever be able to understand sufficiently—on the basis of ex- perience—what it means to 'have killed' one's self.

I believe then, that it is no less our fate than our talent that enables us to exercise the profession of psychoanalyst, after being given the chance, through our training analysis, to live with the reality of our past and to give up the most flagrant of our illusions. This means tolerating the knowledge that, to avoid losing the object-love (the love of the first object), we were compelled to gratify our parents' unconscious needs at the cost of our own self-realization. It also means being able to experience the rebellion and mourning aroused by the fact that our parents were not available to fulfil our primary narcissistic needs. If we have never lived through this despair and the resulting narcissistic rage, and have therefore never been able to work through it, we can be in danger of transferring this situation, which then would have remained unconscious, on to our patients. It would not be surprising if our unconscious anger should find no better way than once more to make use of a weaker person and to make him take the unavailable parents' place. This can be done most easily with one's own children, or with patients, who at times are as dependent on their analysts as children are on their parents. An analytically talented patient, one with 'antennae' for his analyst's unconscious, reacts promptly. He will present the analyst with a complete picture of his 'Oedipus complex', with all the affects and insights that are required. The only disadvantage is that we then have to deal with an 'as-if' Oedipus complex, a defence against the patient's real feelings. Not until he has been given time and space to develop his 'true self', to let it speak and to listen to it, can the unknown, unique history of his Oedipal vicissitudes be unfolded, affecting both patient and analyst, because it is the painfully discovered truth.

This is true not only for the Oedipus complex, but for everything. Such an analysand will quickly 'feel' himself autonomous, and he will react accordingly if he senses that it is important to his analyst to have analysands who soon become autonomous and behave with self-confidence. He can do that, he can do anything that is expected of him. But as this 'autonomy' is not genuine, it soon ends in depression. True autonomy is preceded by the experience of being dependent, first on partners, then on the analyst, and finally on the primary objects. True liberation can only be found beyond the deep ambivalence of infantile dependence.*

The patient satisfies his analyst's narcissistic wish for approval, echo, understanding, and for being taken seriously when he presents material that fits his analyst's knowledge, concepts and skills, and therefore also his expectations. In this way the analyst exercises the same sort of unconscious manipulation as that to which he was exposed as a child. He has, of course, long since seen through conscious manipulation and freed himself from it. He has also learned to say no and to stand up for his own opinions and carry them through. But a child can never see through *unconscious manipulation*. It is like the air he breathes; he knows no other, and it appears to him to be the only normal possibility.

One analysand, for example, could never be sad nor cry as a child, without being aware that he was making his beloved mother unhappy and very unsure of herself, for 'cheerfulness' was the trait that had saved her life in her own childhood. Her children's tears threatened her equilibrium. The extremely sensitive child felt within himself a whole abyss warded off by his mother, who had been in a concentration camp as a child, but had never spoken about it. Not until her son was grown up and could ask her questions did she tell him that she was one of eighty children who had to watch their

* The theses formulated here are based on my own experience, but they can also be illustrated by the experiences of other analysts; cf. case material presented by M. Stern, 1972, and Masud Khan, 1974.

parents going into the gas chambers, and not one child had cried. Throughout his childhood this son had tried to be cheerful and could express his 'true self', his feelings, and inklings only in obsessive perversions, which seemed alien, shameful and incomprehensible to him until he came into analysis.

The shaming nature of perversions and obsessional behaviour can often be understood as the introjection of the parents' shocked reaction to their child's natural, instinctual behaviour. 'Normal' sexual fulfilment no longer evokes horror in the introjected mother as it formerly did in the real one, but perverted behaviour is sure to do so.

One is totally defenceless against this sort of manipulation in childhood. The tragedy is that the parents too have no defence against it, since they do not know what is happening, and even if they have some inkling can do nothing to change it. Their conscious aims are genuinely quite different, even giving every possible support; but unconsciously the parents' childhood tragedy is continued in their children.*

Another example may illustrate this more clearly: a father, who as a child had often been frightened by the anxiety attacks of his periodically schizophrenic mother, without ever receiving an explanation, enjoyed telling his beloved small daughter gruesome stories. He laughed at her fears and afterwards always comforted her with the words: 'But it is only a made-up story. You don't need to be scared, you are here with me.' In this

* For the tragic aspects of psychoanalysis see Roy Schafer, 1972.

way he could manipulate his child's fear and have the feeling of being strong. His conscious wish was to give the child something valuable that he himself had been deprived of, namely protection, comfort and explanations. But what he unconsciously handed on was his own childhood fear, the expectation of disaster, and the unanswered question (also from his childhood): Why does the person whom I love and who loves me frighten me so much?

Probably everybody has a more or less concealed inner chamber that he hides even from himself and in which the props of his childhood drama are to be found. These props may be his secret delusion, a secret perversion, or quite simply the unmastered aspects of his childhood suffering. The only ones who will certainly gain entrance to this hidden chamber are his children. With them new life comes into it, and the drama is continued. All the same, when he was a child he hardly had a chance to play freely with these props, his role merged into his life. And so he could not take any memories of such playing with him for later, except through unconscious repetition in analysis, when he might begin to ask questions about his role. The props may well have frightened him at times. Understandably, he could not connect them with the familiar figures of father or mother, for, after all, they represented the split-off, unintegrated part of the parents. But the child cannot experience this contradiction consciously; he simply accepts everything and, at the most, develops symptoms. Then, in analysis, the feelings emerge: feelings of terror, of despair and rebellion, of mistrust but—if it is possible to reconstruct the parents' vicissitudes—also of compassion and reconciliation.

Can it be an accident that Heinrich Pestalozzi—who was fatherless from his sixth year onward and emotionally neglected despite the presence of his mother and of a nurse—had the idea of bringing up his only son according to Rousseau's methods, although he was capable, on the other hand, of giving orphan children genuine warmth and 'fatherliness'? This son finally grew up neglected, as a ten-year-old was considered to be mentally defective, caused Pestalozzi much pain and guilt feelings, and then died at the age of thirty (H. Ganz, 1966;* M. Lavater-Sloman, 1977). It was also Pestalozzi who is reputed to have said: 'You can drive the devil out of your garden but you will find him again in the garden of your son.' In psychoanalytic terms, one could say that it is the split-off and unintegrated parts of his parents that have been introjected by the child.

---

* In H. Ganz we can read: 'Jakobli is to have a garden of his own to look after, set plants in, "collecting chrysalis and beetles in an orderly, exact, and industrious manner . . . what a bridle for indolence and wildness." Jakobli is now three and a half.

'It would be about a year later, on the occasion of his father's name-day, that Jakobli, who could not write, "half singing, half murmuring", gaily dictated to his mother: "I wish my dear Papa . . . that you should see a lot more and I thank you a hundred thousand times for your goodness. . . . that you have brought me up so joyfully and lovingly. Now I shall speak from my heart. . . . it makes me terribly happy, if you can say I have brought my son up to happiness. . . . I am his joy and his happiness, then shall I first give thanks for what you have done in my life." ' (p. 53)

CONCLUDING REMARKS

The more insight one gains into the unintentional and unconscious manipulation of children by their parents, the fewer illusions one has about the possibility of changing the world or of prophylaxis against neurosis. It seems to me that if we can do anything at all, it is to work through our narcissistic problems and reintegrate our split-off aspects to such an extent that we no longer have any need to manipulate our patients according to our theories but can allow them to become what they really are. Only after painfully experiencing and accepting our own truth can we be relatively free from the hope that we might still find an understanding, empathic mother—perhaps in a patient—who then would be at our disposal.

This temptation should not be underestimated; our own mother seldom or never listened to us with such rapt attention as our patients usually do, and she never revealed her inner world to us so clearly and honestly as our patients do at times. However, the never-ending work of mourning can help us not to lapse into this illusion. A mother such as we once urgently needed—empathic and open, understanding and understandable, available and usable, transparent, clear, without unintelligible contradictions—such a mother was never ours, indeed she could not exist; for every mother carries with her a bit of her 'unmastered past', which she unconsciously hands on to her child. Each mother can only react empathically to the extent that she has become free of her own childhood, and she is forced to react without empathy to the extent that, by denying the vicissitudes of her early life, she wears invisible chains.

But what do exist are children like this: intelligent, alert, attentive, extremely sensitive, and (because they are completely attuned to her well-being) entirely at the mother's disposal and ready for her use. Above all, they are transparent, clear, reliable and easy to manipulate—as long as their true self (their emotional world) remains in the cellar of the transparent house in which they have to live—sometimes until puberty or until they come to analysis, and very often until they have become parents themselves.

In Alphonse Daudet's *Lettres de mon moulin* I have found a story that may sound rather bizarre, but nevertheless has much in common with what I have presented here. I shall summarize the story briefly.

Once upon a time there was a child who had a golden brain. His parents only discovered this by chance when he injured his head and gold instead of blood flowed out. They then began to look after him carefully and would not let him play with other children for fear of being robbed. When the boy was grown up and wanted to go out into the world, his mother said: 'We have done so much for you, we ought to be able to share your wealth.' Then her son took a large piece of gold out of his brain and gave it to his mother. He lived in great style with a friend who, however, robbed him one night and ran away. After that the man resolved to guard his secret and to go out to work, because his reserves were visibly dwindling.

One day he fell in love with a beautiful girl who loved him too, but no more than the beautiful clothes he gave her so lavishly. He married her and was very happy, but after two years she died and he spent the rest of his wealth on her funeral, which had to be splendid. Once, as he was creeping through the streets, weak, poor, and unhappy, he saw a beautiful little pair of boots that would just have done for his wife. He forgot that she was dead—perhaps because his emptied brain no longer worked—and entered the shop to buy the boots. But in that very moment he fell, and the shopkeeper saw a dead man lying on the ground.

Daudet, who was to die from an illness of the spinal cord, wrote below the end of this story:

This story sounds as though it were invented, but it is true from beginning to end. There are people who have to pay for the smallest things in life with their very substance and their spinal cord. That is a constantly recurring pain, and then when they are tired of suffering . . .

Does not mother love belong to the 'smallest', but also indispensable, things in life, for which many people paradoxically have to pay by giving up their living selves?

2

Depression and Grandiosity as Related Forms of Narcissistic Disturbance

Over the years, my analytic work has included many initial consultations with people seeking advice in looking for an analyst, whom I saw for one or two sessions. In these short encounters, the tragedy of an individual destiny can often be seen with moving clarity and intensity. What is described as depression and experienced as emptiness, futility, fear of impoverishment, and loneliness can often be recognized as the tragedy of the loss of the self, or alienation from the self, from which many suffer in our generation and society. Through the years of reconstructive work with my analysands, I think I have come closer to the childhood origins of this alienation from the self.

The observations of early mother–child interaction, recorded by Mahler, Spitz, and Robertson, confirm my suppositions. On reading Winnicott, I felt on familiar ground and encouraged to continue along this path. Finally, Kohut's studies on narcissism, especially his concept of narcissistic cathexis, helped me to conceptualize the relationships I had discovered.

I shall dispense here with the metapsychological language of structure theory and try to develop the connections I want to show on the basis of the mother–child relationship. Obviously, a large part of the events I shall describe take place intraphysically, but every internalization is preceded by an object relationship and its language seems to me emotionally more true and, for some analysts, easier to understand.

THE VICISSITUDES OF NARCISSISTIC NEEDS

We cathect an object narcissistically, according to Kohut (1971), when we experience it not as the centre of its own activity but as a part of ourselves. If the object does not behave as we expect or wish, we may at times be immeasurably disappointed or offended, almost as if an arm ceased to obey us or a function that we take for granted (such as memory) lets us down. This sudden loss of control may also lead to an intense narcissistic rage.

This sort of attitude is met far more frequently in adults than one might imagine, however much we like to regard it as pathological, unrealistic or egocentric. Yet, in the earliest stage of our life, this is the only attitude possible. Not only during the phase of primary narcissism (the symbiotic phase) but also after the gradual separation between self- and object-representations does the mother normally remain a narcissistically cathected object, a function of the developing individual.

Every child has a legitimate narcissistic need to be noticed, understood, taken seriously, and respected by his mother. In the first weeks and months of life he needs to have the mother at his disposal, must be able to use her and to be mirrored by her. This is beautifully illustrated in one of Winnicott's images: the mother gazes at the baby in her arms, and baby gazes at his mother's face and finds himself therein. . . . provided that the mother is really looking at the unique, small, helpless being and not projecting her own introjects on to the child, nor her own expectations, fears, and plans for the child. In that case, the child would not find himself in his mother's face but rather the mother's own predicaments. This child would remain without a mirror, and for the rest of his life would be seeking this mirror in vain.

HEALTHY NARCISSISM

If a child is lucky enough to grow up with a mirroring mother, who allows herself to be cathected narcissistically, who is at the child's disposal—that is, a mother who allows herself to be 'made use of' as a function of the child's narcissistic development, as Mahler (1968) says—then a healthy self-feeling can gradually develop in the growing child. Ideally, this mother should also provide the necessary emotional climate and understanding for the child's needs. But even a mother who is not especially warm-hearted can make this development possible, if she only refrains from preventing it. This enables the child to acquire from other people what the mother lacks. Various investigations have shown the incredible ability that a healthy child displays in making use of the smallest affective 'nourishment' (stimulation) to be found in his surroundings.

I understand a healthy self-feeling to mean the unquestioned certainty that the feelings and wishes one experiences are a part of one's self. This certainty is not something one can gain upon reflection; it is there like one's own pulse, which one does not notice as long as it functions normally.

This automatic, natural contact with his own emotions and wishes gives an individual strength and *self-esteem*. He may live out his feelings, be sad, despairing, or in need of help, without fear of making the introjected mother insecure. He can allow himself to be afraid when he is threatened, or angry when his wishes are not fulfilled. He knows not only what he does not want but also what he wants and is able to express this, irrespective of whether he will be loved or hated for it.

I will now enumerate some characteristics of a successful narcissistic development but would like to make it clear that here, as also later on, I am describing constructions of phenomena that are only approximated in reality. Instead of 'healthy narcissism', it would also be possible to speak of inner freedom and vitality.

• Aggressive impulses could be neutralized because they did not upset the confidence and self-esteem of the parents.

- Strivings toward autonomy were not experienced as an attack.
- The child was allowed to experience and express 'ordinary' impulses (such as jealousy, rage, defiance) because his parents did not require him to be 'special', for instance, to represent their own ethical attitudes.
- There was no need to please anybody (under optimal conditions), and the child could develop and exhibit whatever was active in him during each developmental phase.
- He could use his parents because they were independent of him.
- These preconditions enabled him to separate successfully self- and object-representations.
- Because the child was able to display ambivalent feelings, he could learn to regard both his self and the object as 'both good and bad', and did not need to split off the 'good' from the 'bad' object.
- Object-love was made possible because the parents also loved the child as a separate object.
- Provided there were phase-appropriate and non-traumatic frustrations, the child was able to integrate his narcissistic needs and did not have to resort to repression or splitting.
- This integration made their transformation possible, as well as the development of a drive-regulating matrix, based on the child's own trial-and-error experiences.

NARCISSISTIC DISTURBANCE

What happens if the mother not only is unable to take over the narcissistic functions for the child but also, as very often happens, is herself in need of narcissistic supplies? Quite unconsciously, and despite her own good intentions, the mother then tries to assuage her own narcissistic needs through her child, that is, she cathects him narcissistically. This does not rule out strong affection. On the contrary, the mother often loves her child as her self-object, passionately, but not in the way he needs to be loved. Therefore, the continuity and constancy that would be so important for the child are missing, among other things, from this love. Yet, what is missing above all is the framework within which the child could experience his feelings and his emotions. Instead, he develops something the mother needs, and this certainly saves his life (the mother's or the father's love) at the time, but it nevertheless may prevent him, throughout his life, from being himself.

In such cases the natural narcissistic needs appropriate to the child's age that are here described cannot be integrated into the developing personality. They are split off, partially repressed, and retain their early, archaic form, which makes their later integration still more difficult.

'It is the specific unconscious need of the mother;' writes Mahler (1968), 'that activates, out of the infant's infinite potentialities, those in particular that create for each mother "the child" who reflects her own unique and individual needs.' In other words,. the mother communicates a 'mirrored framework' in infinitely varied ways to which the infant's primitive self accommodates itself. If the mother's 'primary occupation with her child—her mirroring function during the period of early childhood—is unpredictable, insecure, anxiety-ridden or hostile, or if her confidence in herself as a mother is shaken, then the child has to face the period of individuation without having a reliable framework for emotional checking to his symbiotic partner. The result is a disturbance in his primitive self-feeling.

With two exceptions, the mothers of all my patients had a narcissistic disturbance, were extremely insecure, and often suffered from depression. The child, an only one or often the first-born, was the narcissistically cathected object. What these mothers had once failed to find in their own mothers they were able to find in their children: someone at their disposal who can be used as an echo, who can be controlled, is completely centred on them, will never desert them, and offers full attention and admiration. If the child's demands become too great (as once did those of her own mother), she is no longer so defenceless and will not allow herself to be tyrannized: she can bring the child up in such a way that he neither cries nor disturbs her. At last she can make sure that she receives consideration and respect.

Let me illustrate this with an example. A patient who was the mother of four children had only scanty memories of her own mother. At the beginning of the treatment, she described her as an affectionate, warm-hearted woman who spoke to her 'openly about her own troubles' at an early age, who was very concerned for her own children, and sacrificed herself for her family. She must have had the ability to empathize with other people, for she was often asked for advice by others within the sect to which the family belonged. The patient reported that her mother had always been especially proud of her. The mother was now old and an invalid, and the patient was very concerned about her health. She often dreamed that something had happened to her mother and woke up with great anxiety.

During the further course of the analysis and as a consequence of the emotions that arose in the transference, this picture of her mother changed. Above all, when the period of toilet-training entered the analysis, she experienced her mother in me as domineering, demanding, controlling, manipulative, bad, cold, stupid, petty, obsessional, touchy, easily offended, overwrought, false, and hard to please. Even if this picture contained the projection of her long dammed-up anger, many childhood memories of her mother did in fact include these characteristics.

It was only in the course of the analysis, during which she re-enacted a great deal from her childhood, that this patient could discover what her mother was really like, through observing her own relationship to her children. Towards the end, she felt that when her mother had felt insecure in relation to her, she had in fact often been cold and had treated her badly. Her mother's anxious concern for the child had been a reaction formation to ward off her aggression and envy. Since the mother had often been humiliated as a child, she needed to be valued by her daughter. Gradually, the two pictures of the loving mother and of the wicked witch were united into that of a single human being whose weakness, insecurity and oversensitivity made it necessary for her to have her child at her disposal. The mother, who apparently functioned well, was herself basically still a child in her relationship to her own child. The daughter, on the other hand, took over the understanding and caring role until she discovered, with her own children, the demanding child within herself who seemed compelled to press others into her service.

Not all children of narcissistically deprived mothers have to suffer from such a disturbance. The siblings can usually obtain a certain freedom when one child has already accepted this role. Children who have a nurse or another stranger caring for them from the beginning are usually freer to develop in their own way because they are less often the object of narcissistic cathexis.

In his novel *Le Lys dans la vallée*, Honoré de Balzac described his childhood. His mother preferred his brother, gave Honoré first into the care of a nurse and then sent him away to school. He suffered greatly and all his life courted his mother in the guise of different women. But perhaps he was fortunate that this mother did not use him as a glorification of herself. The very hopelessness of his wooing gave him the possibility of developing his own emotional wealth and the ability to freely develop his exceptional capacity for suffering. Perhaps the same is true of Vincent Van Gogh, whose mother, throughout her life, mourned and idealized the first Vincent who had died very young. (Nagera, 1967)

The narcissistically cathected child has the chance to develop his intellectual capacities undisturbed, but not the world of his emotions, and this will have far-reaching consequences for his well-being. Now his intellect will assume a supportive function of enormous value in strengthening his defence mechanism, but hidden behind that, his narcissistic disturbance may grow deeper.

We may, in fact, find various mixtures and nuances of narcissistic disturbances. For the sake of clarity, I shall try to describe two extreme forms, of which I consider one to be the reverse of the other—grandiosity and depression. Behind manifest grandiosity, there constantly lurks depression, and behind a depressive mood there often hide unconscious (or conscious but split off) fantasies of grandiosity. In fact, grandiosity is the defence against depression, and depression is the defence against the deep pain over the loss of the self.

Grandiosity

The person who is 'grandiose' is admired everywhere and needs this admiration; indeed, he cannot live without it. He must excel brilliantly in everything he undertakes, which he surely is capable of doing (otherwise he just does not attempt it). He, too, admires himself—for his qualities: his beauty, cleverness, talents; and for his success and achievements. Woe betide if one of these fails him, for then the catastrophe of a severe depression is imminent. It is usually considered normal that sick or aged people who have suffered the loss of much of their health and vitality, or, for example, women at the time of the menopause, should become depressive. There are, however, other personalities who can tolerate the loss of beauty, health, youth, or loved ones, and although they mourn them they do so without depression. In contrast, there are those with great gifts, often precisely the most gifted,

56

who suffer from severe depression. One is free from depression when self-esteem is based on the authenticity of one's own feelings and not on the possession of certain qualities.

The collapse of self-esteem in a 'grandiose' person will show clearly how precariously that self-esteem had been hanging in the air—'hanging from a balloon', a female patient once dreamed. That balloon flew up very high in a good wind but then suddenly got a hole and soon lay like a little rag on the ground. . . . For nothing genuine that could have given strength and support later on had ever been developed.

The 'grandiose' person's partners (including sexual partners) are also narcissistically cathected. Others are there to admire him, and he himself is constantly occupied, body and soul, with gaining that admiration. This is how his torturing dependence shows itself. The childhood trauma is repeated: he is always the child whom his mother admires, but at the same time he senses that so long as it is his qualities that are being admired, he is not loved for the person he really is at any given time. In the parents' feelings, dangerously close to pride in their child, shame is concealed—lest he should fail to fulfil their expectations.

In a field study conducted at Chestnut Lodge, Maryland, in 1954, the family backgrounds of twelve patients suffering from manic-depressive psychoses were examined. The results strongly confirm the conclusions I have reached, by other means, about the aetiology of depression, and, I believe, of narcissistic disturbances as a whole.

All the patients came from families who were socially isolated and felt themselves to be too little respected in their neighborhood. They therefore made special efforts to increase their prestige with their neighbors through conformity and outstanding achievements. The child who later became ill had been assigned a special role in this effort. He was supposed to guarantee the family honor, and was loved only in proportion to the degree to which he was able to fulfil the demands of this family ideal by *means of his special abilities, talents, his beauty, etc.* If he failed, he was punished by being cold-shouldered or thrown out of the family group, and by the knowledge that he had brought great shame on his people [my italics]. (M. Eicke-Spengler, 1977, p. 1104)

I have found a similar social isolation in the families of my patients but saw this as the result rather than the cause of the parents' narcissistic disturbance.

It is thus impossible for the grandiose person to cut the tragic link between admiration and love. In his compulsion to repeat he seeks insatiably for admiration, of which he never gets enough because admiration is not the same thing as love. It is only a substitute gratification of the primary needs for respect, understanding, and being taken seriously—needs that have remained unconscious.

When Kernberg (1974) spoke of the remarkably strong envy shown by narcissistically disturbed patients in a discussion group at the Paris Congress in 1973, he remarked, almost as an aside: 'These people are envious of everything, even of other people's object relations.' Do we not have to assume that it is precisely there that the unconscious roots of their excessive envy are to be found? A patient once spoke of the feeling of always having to walk on stilts. Is somebody who always has to walk on stilts not bound to be constantly envious of those who can walk on their own legs, even if they seem to him to be smaller and more 'ordinary' than he is himself? And is he not bound to carry pent-up rage within himself, against those who have made him afraid to walk without stilts? Thus envy of other things can come about as the result of the defence mechanism of displacement. Basically, he is envious of healthy people because they do not have to make a constant effort to earn admiration, and because they do not have to do something in order to impress, one way or the other, but are free to be 'average'.

Manifest grandiosity, especially in the erotic sphere, is often described as 'phallic narcissism'. The women with the structure and pathogenesis described here usually attained their 'special position' in the sexual sphere during the Oedipal phase or even earlier (in cases where the mother was emotionally replaced by the father). They had been specially predestined to this by their development during the pre-Oedipal period as narcissistic showpieces of the mother. If seductive behaviour on the father's part is added, then the woman is forced, by the compulsion to repeat, to go on looking for a special position in her relationships to men. She also has to repress the painful rivalry of the Oedipal triangle in order to maintain the fantasy of her favoured position with her father. The inability to develop genuine object-love is also narcissistically mortifying, since it is part of her ambition to be a complete woman—that is, capable of loving. Paradoxically, she owes this to her introjected and subsequently transformed mother as well.

Things may be simpler for the so-called phallic man. He is his mother's special son and, in the seduction situation, her preferred sexual object. The 'phallic man' must be a really splendid fellow if he wants to feel like a man at all. However, as soon as he has to be something specific and is not allowed to be what he really is, he loses, understandably, his sense of self. He then tries all the more to blow up his self-esteem, which again leads to narcissistic weakening, and so on, *ad infinitum*. Fellini's *Casanova* portrayed this person and his anguish most impressively.

The grandiose person is never really free, first, because he is excessively dependent on admiration from the object, and second, because his self-respect is dependent on qualities, functions and achievements that can suddenly fail.

Depression as the Reverse of Grandiosity

Among the patients I have known, depression was coupled with grandiosity in many ways.

1. Depression sometimes appeared when grandiosity broke down as a result of sickness, disablement, or ageing. The source of external narcissistic supplies, for example, gradually dried up in the case of an unmarried woman as she grew older. She no longer received, from men, constant confirmation of her attractiveness, which earlier had a directly supportive function as a substi-

tute for the missing mirroring by her mother. Super-
ficially, her despair about getting old seemed to be due
to the absence of sexual contacts but, at a deeper level,
early pre-Oedipal fears of being abandoned (stemming
from the symbiotic phase) were now aroused, and this
woman had no new conquests with which to counteract
them. All her substitute mirrors were broken, and she
again stood helpless and confused, as the small girl
once did before her mother's face in which she did not
find herself but her mother's confusion.

The so-called phallic, narcissistic men can experience
their ageing in a similar way, even if a new love affair
may seem to create the illusion of their youth for a time
and in this way may introduce brief manic phases into
the early stages of the depression caused by their
ageing.

2. This combination of alternating phases of grandiosity and depression can be seen in many other people.
They are the two sides of the medal that could be
described as the 'false self', a medal that was actually
once given for achievements.

An actor, for example, at the height of his success, can
play before an enthusiastic audience and experience
feelings of heavenly greatness and almightiness.
Nevertheless, his sense of emptiness and futility, even
of shame and anger, can return the next morning if his
happiness the previous night was due not only to his
creative activity in playing and expressing the part but
also, and above all, was rooted in the substitute
satisfaction of old needs for echoing, mirroring, and
being seen and understood. If his success the previous

night only serves as the denial of childhood frustrations, then, like every substitute, it can only bring momentary satiation. In fact, true satiation is no longer possible, since the right time for that now lies irrevocably in the past. The former child no longer exists, nor do the former parents. The present parents—if they are still alive–are now old and dependent, have no longer any power over their son, are delighted with his success and with his infrequent visits. In the present, the son enjoys success and recognition, but these things cannot offer him more than they are, they cannot fill the old gap. Again, as long as he can deny this with the help of illusion, that is, the intoxication of success, the old wound cannot heal. Depression leads him close to his wounds, but only the mourning for what he has missed, *missed at the crucial time*, can lead to real healing.*

3. Continuous performance of outstanding achievements may sometimes enable an individual to maintain the illusion of constant attention and availability of

* Let me cite a remark by Igor Stravinsky as an example of successful mourning: 'I am convinced that it was my misfortune that my father was spiritually very distant from me and that even my mother had no love for me. When my oldest brother died unexpectedly (without my mother transferring her feelings from him onto me, and my father, also, remaining as reserved as ever), I resolved that one day I would show them. Now this day has come and gone. No one remembers this day but me, who am its only remaining witness.' This is in marked contrast to the statement by Samuel Beckett: 'One could say that I had a happy childhood, although I showed little talent for being happy. My parents did all that can be done to make a child happy, but I often felt very lonely.' Here the childhood drama has been fully introjected, and idealization of the parents was maintained with the help of denial, yet the boundless isolation of his childhood found expression in Beckett's plays. (For both quotations see H. Müller-Braunschweig, 1974.)

his self-object (whose absence, in his early childhood, he must now deny just as much as his own emotional reactions). Such a person is usually able to ward off threatening depression with increased displays of brilliance, thereby deceiving both himself and those around him. However, he quite often chooses a marriage partner who either already has strong depressive traits or at least, within their marriage, unconsciously takes over and enacts the depressive components of the grandiose partner. This means that the depression is outside. The grandiose one can look after his 'poor' partner, protect him like a child, feel himself to be strong and indispensable, and thus gain another supporting pillar for the building of his own personality, which actually has no secure foundations and is dependent on the supporting pillars of success, achievement, 'strength', and above all, of denying the emotional world of his childhood.

4. Finally, depression can be experienced as a constant and overt dejection that appears to be unrelated to grandiosity. However, the repressed or split-off fantasies of grandiosity of the depressive are easily discovered, for example, in his moral masochism. He has especially severe standards that apply only to himself. In other people he accepts without question thoughts and actions that, in himself, he would consider mean or bad when measured against his high ego ideal. Others are allowed to be 'ordinary', but that he can never be.

Although the outward picture of depression is quite the

opposite of that of grandiosity and has a quality that expresses the tragedy of the loss of self to a great extent, they have the same roots in the narcissistic disturbance. Both are indications of an inner prison, because the grandiose and the depressive individuals are compelled to fulfil the introjected mother's expectations: whereas the grandiose person is her successful child, the depressive sees himself as a failure.

They have many points in common:

- A 'false self' that has led to the loss of the potential 'true self'
- A fragility of self-esteem that is based on the possibility of realizing the 'false self' because of lack of confidence in one's own feelings and wishes
- Perfectionism, a very high ego ideal
- Denial of the rejected feelings (the missing of a shadow in the reflected image of Narcissus)
- A preponderance of narcissistic cathexes of objects
- An enormous fear of loss of love and therefore a great readiness to conform
- Envy of the healthy
- Strong aggression that is split off and therefore not neutralized
- Oversensitivity
- A readiness to feel shame and guilt
- Restlessness

Thus depression can be understood as a sign of the loss of the self and consists of a denial of one's own emotional reactions and feelings. This denial begins in the service of an absolutely essential adaptation during childhood, to avoid losing the object's love. Thereafter it continues under the influence of the introjects. For

this reason depression indicates a very early disturbance. Right at the beginning, in infancy, such persons
have suffered from a deficiency in certain affective
areas that are necessary for stable self-confidence. From
the reconstructions available through analyses, I have
gained the impression that there are children who have
not been free to experience the very earliest feelings,
such as discontent, anger, rage, pain, even hunger and,
of course, enjoyment of their own bodies.

Discontent and anger had aroused uncertainty in the
mother over her maternal role, pain had made her
anxious. Her children's enjoyment of their bodies
sometimes aroused her envy, sometimes her shame
about 'what other people would think', or it disturbed
the mother's reaction formations (Miller, 1971). Thus,
under certain circumstances, a child may learn very
early what he is not allowed to feel, lest he run the risk
of losing his mother's love.

A patient in her fourth year of analysis came to a
session several weeks after the birth of her third child
and told me how free and alive she felt with this baby,
quite in contrast to the way she had felt with the two
earlier ones. With them she had constantly felt that
excessive demands were being made upon her, that she
was a prisoner, and that the baby was taking advantage
of and 'exploiting' her. Thus she rebelled against his
justified demands and, at the same time, felt that this
was very bad of her: as in depression, she was separated
from her true self. She thought these earlier reactions
might have been rebellion against her mother's demands, for this time she was experiencing nothing of

this sort. The love she had then struggled to feel now came of its own accord. She could enjoy her unity with this child and with herself. Then she spoke of her mother in the following words:

'I was the jewel in my mother's crown. She often said: "Maja can be relied upon, she will cope." And I did cope, I brought up the smaller children for her so that she could get on with her professional career. She became more and more famous, but I never saw her happy. How often I longed for her in the evenings. The little ones cried and I comforted them but I myself never cried. Who would have wanted a crying child? I could only win my mother's love if I was competent, understanding, and controlled, if I never questioned her actions nor showed her how much I missed her; that would have limited her freedom, which she needed so much. It would have turned her against me. At that time, nobody ever would have thought that this quiet, competent, useful Maja could be so lonely and have suffered so much. What could I do but be proud of my mother and help her? The deeper the hole in my mother's heart was, the bigger the jewels in her crown needed to be. My poor mother needed these jewels because, at bottom, all her activity served only to suppress something in herself, perhaps a longing, I don't know . . . . Perhaps *she* would have discovered it if she had been fortunate enough to be a mother in more than a biological sense. It is not her fault. She tried so hard. But she had not been given the gift.

'And how all of this repeated itself with Peter! How many empty hours my child had to spend with the maids so that I could get my diploma, which only took me further away from him and from myself. How often I deserted him without seeing what I was doing to him, because I had never been able to experience

66

my own sense of being deserted? Only now do I begin to realize what motherhood without crown or jewels or a halo can be like.'

A German women's magazine (which tries to speak openly of truths that have been tabooed) published a reader's letter in which the tragic story of her experience of motherhood was told without camouflage. It is in the nature of the problem that she could not really experience either her own tragedy or that of her child, since her own emotionally inaccessible childhood was the real beginning of the story. Her report ends with the following passage:

And then the breast-feeding! The baby was put to the breast all wrong and soon my nipples were all bitten. God, how that hurt. Just two hours and then it was back: another one . . . the same . . . while it was sucking there, I was crying and swearing above it. It was so terrible that soon I couldn't eat any more and had a temperature of 40° [Celsius]. Then I was allowed to wean and suddenly felt better. It was a long time before I noticed any maternal feelings. I wouldn't have minded if the baby had died. And everybody expected me to be happy. In despair I telephoned a friend who said that I'd get fond of him in time through being busy with him and having him around all the time. But that did not happen either. I only *began to be fond* of him when I could go back to work and only saw him when I came home, as a *distraction and toy*, so to speak. But quite honestly, a little dog would have done just as well. Now that he is gradually getting bigger and I see that *I can train him and that he is devoted to me and trusts me*, I am beginning to develop *tender feelings* for him and am glad that he is there [my italics].

I have written all this because I think it is a good thing that someone should, at last, say that there is no such thing as mother love—not to speak of a maternal instinct. (*Emma*, July 1977)

THE LEGEND OF NARCISSUS

The legend of Narcissus actually tells us the tragedy of the narcissistic disturbance. Narcissus sees his reflection in the water and falls in love with his own beautiful face, of which his mother was surely proud. The nymph Echo answers the young man's calls because she is in love with his beauty, just as their mothers are with our patients. Echo's answering calls deceive Narcissus. His reflection deceives him as well, since it shows only his perfect, wonderful side and not his other parts. His back view, for instance, and his shadow remain hidden from him; they do not belong to and are cut off from his beloved reflection.

This stage of rapture can be compared with grandiosity, just as the next (the consuming longing for himself) can be likened to depression. Narcissus wanted to be nothing but the beautiful youth. He denied his true self, wanted to be at one with the beautiful picture. This leads to a giving up of himself, to death or, in Ovid's version, to being changed into a flower. This death is the logical consequence of the fixation on the false self. It is not only the 'beautiful', 'good' and pleasant feelings that make us really alive, deepen our existence, and give us

68

crucial insight—but often precisely the unacceptable and unadapted ones from which we would prefer to escape: impotence, shame, envy, jealousy, confusion and mourning. These feelings can be experienced in the analyst's consulting room and grow beyond their archaic form. In this way this room is also a mirror of the analysand's inner world, which is much richer than the 'beautiful countenance'!

Narcissus was in love with his idealized picture, but neither the grandiose nor the depressive 'Narcissus' can really love himself. His passion for his false self not only makes object-love impossible but also love for the one person who is fully entrusted to his care: he, himself.

DEPRESSIVE PHASES DURING ANALYSIS

A grandiose person will only look for an analyst if depressive episodes come to his aid and force him to do so. As long as the grandiose defence is effective, this form of narcissistic disturbance exerts no pressure through visible suffering, except when other members of the family (spouse or children) have to seek psychotherapeutic help for depression or psychosomatic disorders. In our analytic work, we encounter grandiosity that is coupled with depression. On the other hand, we see depression in almost all our patients, either in the form of a manifest illness or in distinct phases of depressive moods. These phases can have different functions.

Depression and Grandiosity

SIGNAL FUNCTION

Every analyst is familiar with sessions when the patient arrives complaining of depression and later leaves the consulting room in tears but much relieved and free from depression. Perhaps this patient now has been able to experience a long-pent-up rage against his mother; or he has been able to express his mistrust of the analyst's superiority, or to feel for the first time his sadness over the many lost years of his life during which he did not really live; or he has vented his anger over the impending holidays and separation from his analyst. It is irrelevant which of these feelings are coming to the fore; the important thing is that they could be experienced. The depression had signalled their proximity but also their denial. The analytic session enabled the feelings to break through and then the depression disappeared. Such a mood can be an indication that parts of the self that had been rejected (feelings, fantasies, wishes, fears) have become stronger without finding discharge in grandiosity.

DENIAL OF SELF

Some patients, while feeling content and understood after having come close to the core of their selves in a session, will organize a party or something else equally unimportant to them at that moment, which will make them feel lonely and inadequate again. After a few days they will complain of self-alienation and emptiness, of again having lost the way to themselves. Here the patient has actively, though unconsciously, provoked a situation that could demonstrate the repetition of what used to happen to him as a child: when he really got a sense of himself in 'play'—feeling creative in Winnicott's sense—he would be asked to do something 'more sensible', to achieve something, and his world, which was just beginning to unfold, would be overthrown. These patients, even as children, probably reacted to this by withdrawing their feelings and by becoming depressed.

THE ACCUMULATION OF STRONG, HIDDEN FEELINGS

Patients who are no longer depressive sometimes still have depressive phases that may last several weeks before strong emotions from their childhood break through. It is as though the depression had held back the effect. When it can be experienced, insight and associations related to the primary objects follow, often accompanied by significant dreams. The patient feels fully alive again until a new depressive phase signals something new. This may be expressed in the following fashion: 'I no longer have a feeling of myself. How could it happen that I should lose myself again? I have no connection with what is within me. It is all hopeless. . . . It will never be any better. Everything is pointless. I am longing for my former sense of being alive.' An aggressive outbreak may follow, with reproaches against the analyst, and only after this outbreak will a new link become clear and new vitality be felt.

Depression and Grandiosity

THE STRUGGLE WITH THE INTROJECTS

During an analysis, there will also be times of depressive moods even after the patient has started to resist the demands of his introjects. He may, for example, resist their demands for achievement, although he has not yet fully freed himself from them. Then he lands again in the cul-de-sac of making pointlessly excessive demands upon himself and he will only become aware of this when a depressive mood rises. This, for instance, may find expression in the following way: 'The day before yesterday I was so happy, my work went easily. I was able to do more work for the exam than I had planned for the whole week. Then I thought I must take advantage of this good mood and do another chapter in the evening. I worked all evening but without any enthusiasm and the next day I couldn't do any more. I felt like such an idiot, nothing stayed in my head. I didn't want to see anyone either, it felt like the depressions I used to have. Then I "turned the pages back" and found where it had begun. I had spoiled my pleasure as soon as I made myself do more and more—but why? Then I remembered how my mother used to say: "You have done that beautifully, now you could surely do this, too. . . ." I got angry and left the books alone. Then, suddenly, I trusted myself to know when I was ready to work again. And, of course, I did, too. But the depression went away sooner—at the point when I realized that I had once again exceeded my limits.'

THE INNER PRISON AND
ANALYTIC WORK

Everyone probably knows from his own experience about depressive moods; they may be expressed as well as hidden by psychosomatic suffering. It is easy to notice, if we pay attention, that they hit a person almost with regularity—whenever he suppresses an impulse or an unwanted emotion. And then, at once, such depressive moods will stifle all spontaneity. If an adult, for example, cannot experience mourning when he loses somebody dear to him but tries to distract himself from his sadness, or if he suppresses and hides from himself his indignation over an idealized friend's behaviour out of fear of losing his friendship, he must reckon with the probability of depression (unless his grandiose defence is constantly at his disposal). When he begins to pay attention to these connections in his analysis, he can benefit from his depression and use it to learn the truth about himself.

A child does not yet have this possibility. He cannot yet see through his mechanism of self-deception and, on the other hand, he is far more threatened than an adult by the intensity of his feelings if he does not have a supportive (holding) empathic environment. Winnicott (1969) compared the infant's emotional world with that of a psychotic, and there is something convincing about this comparison. What these two worlds have in common, in addition to the lack of structuring, is the extreme intensity of feeling that is otherwise only to be

73

found in puberty. Yet, the recollection of the pains of puberty, of not being able to understand or to place our own impulses is usually more accessible than the earliest narcissistic traumata that are often hidden behind the picture of an idyllic childhood or even behind an almost complete amnesia. This is perhaps one reason why adults less often look back nostalgically to the time of their puberty than to that of their childhood. The mixture of longing, expectation, and fear of disappointment, which for most people accompanies the remembrance of the festivities they have known in their childhood, can perhaps be explained by their search for the intensity of feeling they knew in childhood, and cannot regain.

It is precisely because a child's feelings are so strong that they cannot be repressed without serious consequences. The stronger a prisoner is, the thicker the prison walls have to be, which impede or completely prevent later emotional growth.

Once a patient has experienced a few times in the course of his analysis that the breakthrough of intense early-childhood feelings (characterized by the specific quality of non-comprehension) can relieve a long period of depression, this experience will bring about a gradual change in his way of approaching 'undesired' feelings, above all, those of pain. He discovers that he is no longer compelled to follow the former pattern of disappointment, suppression of pain, and depression, since he now has another possibility of dealing with disappointment, namely, that of experiencing pain. In this way he at least gains access to his earlier experiences—to the parts of himself and of his fate that were previously hidden from him.

A patient, in the closing phase of his analysis, expressed it thus:

> 'It was not the beautiful or pleasant feelings that gave me new insight but the ones against which I had fought most strongly: feelings that made me experience myself as shabby, petty, mean, helpless, humiliated, demanding, resentful, or confused; and, above all, sad and lonely. It was precisely through these experiences, which I had shunned for so long, that I became certain that I now understand something about my life, stemming from the core of my being, something that I could not have learned from any book!'

This patient was describing the process of creative insight in psychoanalysis. Interpretations play an important part in this process. They can accompany it, support ('hold') and encourage, but they can also disturb, hamper, and delay, or even prevent it or reduce it to mere intellectual insight. A patient with narcissistic problems is all too ready to give up his own pleasure in discovery and self-expression and accommodate himself to his analyst's concepts—out of fear of losing the latter's affection, understanding, and empathy, for which he has been waiting all his life. Because of his early experiences with his mother, he cannot believe that this need not necessarily be so. If he gives way to this fear and adapts himself, the analysis slides over into the sphere of the 'false self', and the 'true self' remains hidden and undeveloped. It is therefore extremely important that the analyst does not cathect the patient narcissistically, that is, his own needs should not impel him to formulate connections that the patient himself is discovering with the help of his own feelings. Otherwise he is in danger of behaving like a friend who brings some good food to a prisoner in his cell, at the precise moment when that prisoner has the chance to escape, perhaps spending his first night without shelter and hungry, but nevertheless in freedom. Since this step into unknown territory requires a great deal of courage in the first instance, it can happen that the prisoner, comforting himself with his food and shelter, misses his chance and stays in prison.

Recognizing the fragility of a creative process obviously does not mean that the analyst must adopt a mostly silent and hurtful attitude but merely that he must exercise care in this respect. It is possible, for example—provided the analyst respects the analysand's need to discover things for himself—that his compulsion to repeat can be of good service to his creative self-discovery, especially if its indirect communications are understood. This will come about through producing a variety of new situations through which an old, unremembered situation can, for the first time, be consciously experienced in its full tragedy and then finally be mourned. It is part of the dialectic of the mourning process that such experiences both encourage and are dependent on self-discovery (cf. pp. 33–6).

Grandiosity is the counterpart of depression *within* the narcissistic disturbance. The patient can therefore be freed from his depression for a while if the psychotherapist knows how to let the patient share in his own grandeur—that is, when he can enable the patient to feel big and strong as a part of the idealized therapist. The narcissistic disturbance then appears in a different guise for a while, even though it still exists. The achievement of freedom from both forms of narcissistic disturbance in analysis is hardly possible without deeply felt mourning. This ability to mourn, that is, to give up the illusion of his 'happy' childhood, can restore the depressive's vitality and creativity, and (if he comes to analysis at all) free the grandiose person from the exertions of and dependence on his Sisyphean task. If a person is able, during this long process, to experience that he was never 'loved' as a child for what he was but for his achievements, success, and good qualities, and that he sacrificed his childhood for this 'love', this will shake him very deeply but one day he will feel the desire to end this courtship. He will discover in himself a need to live according to his 'true self' and no longer be forced to earn love, a love that at root, still leaves him empty-handed since it is given to the 'false self', which he has begun to relinquish.

The true opposite of depression is not gaiety or absence of pain, but vitality: the freedom to experience spontaneous feelings. It is part of the kaleidoscope of life that these feelings are not only cheerful, 'beautiful' and 'good'; they also can display the whole scale of human experience, including envy, jealousy, rage, disgust, greed, despair and mourning. But this freedom cannot be achieved if the childhood roots are cut off. For a person with narcissistic problems access to the 'true self' is thus only possible when he no longer has to be afraid of the intense 'psychotic' emotional world of his early childhood. Once he has experienced this during the analytic process, it is no longer strange and threatening and need no longer be hidden behind the prison walls of illusion.

A good deal of advice for dealing with the depressive patient (for example, turning his aggression from the inner to the outer world) has a clearly manipulative character. S. Levin, for instance, suggested that one should demonstrate to the patient that 'his hopelessness is not rational' (1965), or make him aware of his 'oversensitivity' (Fischer, 1976). I think that such procedures will only strengthen the 'false self' and emotional conformity—will reinforce the depression, too. If we want to avoid this, we must take *all* the patient's feelings seriously. It is precisely his oversensitivity, shame, and self-reproach (how often a depressive patient knows that he reacts oversensitively and how much he will reproach himself for it) which form a continuous thread throughout his analysis, even before we understand what these feelings really relate to. The more unrealistic such feelings are and the less they fit present reality, the more clearly they show that they are concerned with unremembered situations from the past that are still to be discovered. If, however, the feeling concerned is not experienced but reasoned away, the discovery cannot take place, and depression will be triumphant.

After a long depressive phase, accompanied by suicidal thoughts, a forty-year-old patient was at last able to experience her violent, very early ambivalence in the transference. This was not immediately followed by visible relief but by a period full of mourning and tears. At the end of this period she said:

> 'The world has not changed, there is so much evil and meanness all around me, and I see it even more clearly than before. Nevertheless, for the first time I find life really worth living. Perhaps this is because, for the first time, I have the feeling that I am really living my own life. And that is an exciting adventure. On the other hand, I can understand my suicidal ideas better now, especially those I had in my youth—it seemed pointless to carry on—because in a way I had always been living a life that wasn't mine, that I didn't want, and that I was ready to throw away.'

A SOCIAL ASPECT OF DEPRESSION

One might ask whether adaptation must necessarily lead to depression. It is not possible, and are there not examples, that emotionally conforming individuals may live quite happily? There are indeed such examples, and above all there were more in the past, for depression is a disease of our time. Within a culture that was shielded from other value systems, such as that of orthodox Jewry in the ghetto, or of Negro families in the Southern states a hundred years ago, an adapted individual was not autonomous and did not have his own individual sense of identity (in our sense) that could have given him support; but he did feel supported by the group. The sense of being a 'devout Jew' or a 'loyal slave' gave individuals a measure of security in this world. Of course, there were some exceptions, people for whom that was not sufficient and who were strong enough to break away. Today it is hardly possible for any group to remain so isolated from others who had different values. Therefore it is necessary today for the individual to find his support within himself, if he is not to become the victim of various interests and ideologies. This strength within himself—through access to his own real needs and feelings and the possibility of expressing them—thus becomes crucially important for him on the one hand, and on the other is made enormously more difficult through living in contact with various different value systems. These factors can probably explain the rapid increase of depression in our time and also the general fascination with various groups.

Within the partially adapted child there are latent powers that resist this adaptation. In older children, particularly as they reach puberty, these powers attach themselves to new values, which are often opposed to those of the parents. Thus the youths will create new ideals and will try to put them into practice. Since this attempt is nevertheless not rooted in awareness of his own true needs and feelings, the individual adolescent accepts and conforms to the new ideals in a similar way to that which he previously adopted in relation to his parents. He again gives up and denies his true self in order to be accepted and loved by the heirs of the primary objects (whether in his ego-ideal or in the group). But all that is of little avail against depression.

Depression and Grandiosity

This person is not really himself, nor does he know or love himself: he does everything to make a narcissistically cathected object love him in the way he once, as a child, so urgently needed it. But whatever could not be experienced at the right time in the past can never be attained later on.

There are innumerable examples of this dilemma and I would like to include two of them.

1. A young woman wants to free herself from her patriarchal family in which her mother was completely subjected by the father. She marries a submissive man and seems to behave quite differently from her mother. Her husband allows her to bring her lovers into the house. She does not permit herself any feelings of jealousy or tenderness and wants to have relations with a number of men without any emotional ties, so that she can feel as autonomous as a man. Her need to be 'progressive' goes so far that she allows her partners to abuse and humiliate her as they wish, and she suppresses all her feelings of mortification and anger in the belief that this makes her modern and free from prejudice. In this way she carries over both her childhood obedience and her mother's submissiveness into these relationships. At times she suffers from severe depression.

2. A patient from an African family grew up alone with his mother after his father had died while he was still a very small boy. His mother insists on certain conventions and does not allow the child to be aware of his narcissistic and libidinal needs in any way, let alone express them. On the other hand, she regularly

massages his penis until puberty, ostensibly on medical advice. As an adult her son leaves his mother and her world and marries an attractive European with quite a different background. Is it due to chance or to his unerring instinct that this woman not only torments and humiliates him but also undermines his confidence to an extreme degree, and that he is quite unable to stand up to her or leave her? This sadomasochistic marriage, like the other example, represents an attempt to break away from the parents' social system with the help of another one. The patient was certainly able to free himself from the mother of his adolescence, but he remained emotionally tied to the Oedipal and pre-Oedipal mother whose role was taken over by his wife as long as he was not able to experience the feelings from that period. In his analysis he encountered his original ambivalence. It was terribly painful for him to realize the extent to which he had needed his mother as a child and at the same time had felt abused in his helplessness; how much he had loved her, hated her, and been entirely at her mercy. The patient experienced these feelings after four years of analysis, with the result that he no longer needed his wife's perversions and could separate from her. At the same time he was able to see her far more realistically, including her positive sides.

Depression and Grandiosity

POINTS OF CONTACT WITH SOME
THEORIES OF DEPRESSION

When we conceptualize depression as giving up one's
real self in order to preserve the object, we can find
within this view the main elements of theories of
depression.

1. Freud's factor of *impoverishment* of the ego is, of
course, centrally contained in this concept, allowing for
the fact that, at the time of writing 'Mourning and
Melancholy' (1917), he used the term 'ego' in the sense
in which we now use the term 'self'.

2. What Karl Abraham (1912) described as turning
aggression against the self also is closely related to the
idea of the loss of the self, which I have tried to describe
here. The 'destruction' of one's own feelings, needs, and
fantasies that are unwelcome to the primary object is an
aggressive act against the self. The feelings that are
thus 'killed' by the depressive may vary according to the
child's specific situation—they are not merely linked to
aggressive impulses.

3. W. Joffe and J. Sandler (1965a and 1965b) define
depression as a possible *reaction to psychic pain* caused
by the discrepancy between the actual and the ideal
self-representation. Congruity of these two leads to a
feeling of well-being. In the language of object relations,
that would mean: the ideal self-representation is the
heritage of the primary objects whose approval and love
ensure a sense of well-being, just as their discrepancy
brings the danger of loss of love. If this pain could be

Depression and Grandiosity

risked and experienced, there would be no depression, but for that a supportive ('holding') environment would have been necessary at the crucial time.

4. Finally, according to Edith Jacobson (1971), the conditions for a depressive development arise when loss of the ideal object is denied. Loss here does not merely mean real separation from the self-object, or disappointment that will be traumatic if it is not phase-appropriate, but also the unavailability of the self-object.

The narcissistically disturbed patient did not have a self-object at his disposal during the symbiotic phase, nor a 'usable' object, in Winnicott's sense (1971)—one that would have survived its own destruction. Both the depressive and the grandiose person *deny this reality completely* by living as though the availability of the self-object could still be salvaged: the grandiose person through the illusion of achievement, and the depressive through his constant fear of losing the self-object. Neither of them can accept the truth that this loss or this unavailability has *already happened* in the past, and that *no effort* whatsoever *can ever change this fact*.

3

The Vicious Circle
of Contempt

> Would not God find a way out, some superior
> deception such as the grownups and the
> powerful always contrived, producing one more
> trump card at the last moment, shaming me
> after all, not taking me seriously, humiliating
> me under the damnable mask of kindness?
>
> Herman Hesse, 'A Child's Heart'

HUMILIATION FOR THE CHILD, CONTEMPT
FOR THE WEAK, AND WHERE IT GOES
FROM THERE

EVERYDAY EXAMPLES

While away on a vacation, I was sorting out my
thoughts on the subject of 'contempt' and reading
various notes on this theme that I had made about
individual analytic sessions. Probably sensitized by this

preoccupation, I was more than usually affected by an ordinary scene, in no way spectacular or rare. I shall describe it to introduce my observations, for it illustrates some of the insights I have gained in the course of my analytic work, without any danger of indiscretion.

I was out for a walk and noticed a young couple a few steps ahead, both tall; they had a little boy with them, about two years old, who was running alongside and whining. (We are accustomed to seeing such situations from the adult point of view, but here I want to describe it as it was experienced by the child.) The two had just bought themselves ice-cream bars on sticks from the kiosk and were licking them with enjoyment. The little boy wanted one, too. His mother said affectionately, 'Look, you can have a bite of mine, a whole one is too cold for you.' The child did not want just one bite but held out his hand for the whole ice, which his mother took out of his reach again. He cried in despair, and soon exactly the same thing was repeated with his father: 'There you are, my pet,' said his father affectionately, 'you can have a bite of mine.' 'No, no,' cried the child and ran ahead again, trying to distract himself. Soon he came back again and gazed enviously and sadly up at the two grown-ups, who were enjoying their ice creams contentedly and at one. Time and again he held out his little hand for the whole ice-cream bar, but the adult hand with its treasure was withdrawn again.

The more the child cried, the more it amused his parents. It made them laugh a lot and they hoped to humour him along with their laughter, too: 'Look, it isn't so important, what a fuss you are making.' Once the child sat down on the ground and began to throw little stones over his shoulder in his mother's direction, but then he suddenly got up again and looked around anxiously, making sure that his parents were still there. When his father had completely finished his ice cream, he gave the stick to the child and walked on. The little boy licked the bit of wood expectantly, looked at it, threw it away, wanted to pick it up again but did not do so, and a deep sob of loneliness and disappointment shook his small body. Then he trotted obediently after his parents.

It seemed clear to me that this little boy was not being frustrated in his 'oral drives', for he was given ample opportunity to take a bite; it was his narcissistic needs that were constantly being wounded and frustrated. His wish to hold the ice-cream stick in his hand like the others was not understood, worse still, it was laughed at: they made fun of his needs. He was faced with two giants who were proud of being consistent and also supported each other—while he, quite alone in his distress, obviously could say nothing beyond no, nor could he make himself clear to his parents with his gestures (which were very expressive). He had no advocate.*

Why, indeed, did these parents behave with so little empathy? Why didn't one of them think of eating a little quicker or even of throwing away half his ice cream and

---

* What an unfair situation it is, by the way, when a child is opposed by two big, strong adults, as by a wall; we call it 'consistency in upbringing' when we refuse to let the child complain about one parent to the other.

giving the child his stick with a bit of edible substance? Why did they both stand there laughing, eating so slowly and showing so little concern about the child's obvious distress? They were not unkind or cold parents, the father spoke to his child very tenderly. Nevertheless, at least at this moment, they displayed a lack of empathy. We can only solve this riddle if we manage to see the parents, too, as insecure children—children who have at last found a weaker creature, and in comparison with him they now can feel very strong. What child has never been laughed at for his fears and been told, 'You don't need to be afraid of a thing like that.' And what child will then not feel shamed and despised because he could not assess the danger correctly, and will that little person not take the next opportunity to pass on these feelings to a still smaller child. Such experiences come in all shades and varieties. Common to them all is the sense of strength that it gives the adult to face the weak and helpless child's fear and to have the possibility of controlling fear in another person, while he cannot control his own (cf. pp. 41–2).

No doubt, in twenty years' time, or perhaps earlier, if he has younger siblings, our little boy will replay this scene with the ice cream, but then *he* will be in possession and the other one will be the helpless, envious, weak little creature, whom he then no longer has to carry within himself, but now can split off and project outside himself.

Contempt for those who are smaller and weaker thus is the best defence against a breakthrough of one's own feelings of helplessness: it is an expression of this split-off weakness. The strong person who knows that he, too, carries this weakness within himself, because he has experienced it, does not need to demonstrate his strength through such contempt.

Many adults first become aware of their Oedipal feelings of helplessness, jealousy and loneliness through their own children, since they had no chance to acknowledge and experience these feelings consciously in their childhood (cf. pp. 41–2). I spoke of the patient who was obsessively forced to make conquests with women, to seduce and then to abandon them, until he was at last able to experience in his analysis how he himself had repeatedly been abandoned by his mother. Now he remembered how he had been caught at night outside the locked door of his parents' bedroom and laughed at. Now in the analytic session, is the first time that he consciously experiences the feelings of humiliation and mortification that were then aroused.

The Oedipal suffering that was not lived out can be got rid of by delegating it to one's own children—in much the same way as in the ice-cream scene I have just described: 'You see, we are big, we may do as we like, but for you it is "too cold". You may only enjoy yourself as we do when you get to be big enough.' So, in the Oedipal area, too, it is not the instinctual frustration that is humiliating for the child, but the contempt shown for his instinctual wishes. It may well be that the narcissistic component of Oedipal suffering is commonly accentuated when the parents demonstrate their 'grown-upness' to revenge themselves unconsciously on their child for their own earlier humiliation. In the child's eyes they encounter their own humiliating past, and they must ward it off with the power they now have achieved.

In many societies, little girls suffer additional discrimination because they are girls. Since women, however, have control of the new-born and the infants, these erstwhile little girls can pass on to their children at the most tender age the contempt from which they once suffered. Later, the adult man will idealize his mother, since every human being needs the feeling that he was really loved; but he will despise other women, upon whom he thus revenges himself in place of his mother. And these humiliated adult women, in turn, if they have no other means of ridding themselves of their burden, will revenge themselves upon their own children. This indeed can be done secretly and without fear of reprisals, for the child has no way of telling anyone, except perhaps in the form of a perversion or obsessional neurosis, whose language is sufficiently veiled not to betray the mother.

Contempt is the weapon of the weak and a defence against one's own despised and unwanted feelings. And the fountainhead of all contempt, all discrimination, is the more or less conscious, uncontrolled and secret exercise of power over the child by the adult, which is tolerated by society (except in the case of murder or serious bodily harm). What adults do to their child's spirit is entirely their own affair. For the child is regarded as the parents' property, in the same way as the citizens of a totalitarian state are the property of its government. Until we become sensitized to the small child's suffering, this wielding of power by adults will continue to be a normal aspect of the human condition, for no one pays attention to or takes seriously what is regarded as trivial, since the victims are 'only children'. But in twenty years' time these children will be adults who will have to pay it all back to their own children. They may then fight vigorously against cruelty 'in the world'—and yet they will carry within themselves an experience of cruelty to which they have no access and which remains hidden behind their idealized picture of a happy childhood.

Let us hope that the degree to which this discrimination is persistently transmitted from one generation to the next might be reduced by education and increasing awareness—especially in its more subtle manifestations. Someone who slaps or hits another or knowingly insults him is aware of hurting him. He has some sense of what he is doing. But how often were our parents, and we ourselves towards our own children, unconscious of how painfully, deeply, and lastingly we injured a child's tender, budding self. It is very fortunate when our children are aware of this situation and are able to tell us about it, for this may enable them to throw off the chains of power, discrimination and scorn that have been handed on for generations. When our children can consciously experience their early helplessness and narcissistic rage they will no longer need to ward off their helplessness, in turn, with exercise of power over others. In most cases, however, one's own childhood suffering remains affectively inaccessible and thus forms the hidden source of new and sometimes very subtle humiliation for the next generation. Various defence mechanisms will help to justify this: denial of one's own suffering, rationalization (I owe it to my child to bring him up properly), displacement (it is not my father but my son who is hurting me), idealization (my father's beatings were good for me), and more. And, above all, there is the mechanism of turning passive suffering into active behaviour. The following examples may illustrate how astonishingly similar the ways are in which people protect themselves against their childhood experiences, despite great differences in personality structure and in education.

A thirty-year-old Greek, the son of a peasant and owner of a small restaurant in Western Europe, proudly described how he drinks no alcohol and has his father to thank for this abstinence. Once, at the age of fifteen, he came home drunk and was so severely beaten by his father that he could not move for a week. From that time on he was so averse to alcohol that he could not taste so much as a drop, although his work brought him into constant contact with it. When I heard that he was soon to be married, I asked whether he, too, would beat his children. 'Of course,' he answered, 'beatings are necessary in bringing up a child properly: they are the best way to make him respect you. I would never smoke in my father's presence, for example—and that is a sign of my respect for him.' This man was neither stupid nor uncongenial, but he had little schooling. We might therefore nurse the illusion that education could counteract this process of destroying the spirit.

The Vicious Circle of Contempt

But how does this illusion stand up to the next example, which concerns an educated man?

A talented Czech author is reading from his own works in a town in Western Germany. After the reading there follows a discussion with the audience, during which he is asked questions about his life, which he answers ingenuously. He reports that despite his former support of the Prague Spring he now has plenty of freedom and can frequently travel in the West. He goes on to describe his country's development in recent years. When he is asked about his childhood, his eyes shine with enthusiasm as he talks about his gifted and many-sided father who encouraged his spiritual development and was a true friend. It was only to his father that he could show his first stories. His father was very proud of him, and even when he beat him as punishment for some misdemeanour reported by the mother, he was proud that his son did not cry. Since tears brought extra blows, the child learned to suppress them and was himself proud that he could make his admired father such a great present with his bravery. This man spoke of these regular beatings as though they were the most normal things in the world (as for him, of course, they were), and then he said: 'It did me no harm, it prepared me for life, made me hard, taught me to grit my teeth. And that's why I could get on so well in my profession.'

Contrasting with this Czech author, the film director Ingmar Bergman spoke on a television programme with great awareness and far more understanding of the implications about his own childhood, which he described as one long story of humiliation. He related, for example, that if he wet his trousers he had to wear a red dress all day so that everybody would know what he had done and he would have to be ashamed of himself. Ingmar Bergman was the younger son of a Protestant pastor. In this television interview he described a scene that often occurred during his childhood. His older brother has just been beaten by the father. Now their mother is dabbing his brother's bleeding back with cotton wool. He himself sits watching. Bergman described this scene without apparent agitation, almost coldly. One can see him as a child, quietly sitting and watching. He surely did not run away, nor close his eyes, nor cry. One has the impression that this scene did take place in reality, but at the same time is a covering memory for what *he himself* went through. It is unlikely that only his brother was beaten by their father.

It sometimes happens that patients in analysis are convinced that only their siblings suffered humiliation. Only after years of analysis can they remember, with feelings of rage and helplessness, of anger and indignation, how humiliated and deserted they felt when they were beaten by their beloved father.

Ingmar Bergman, however, had other possibilities, apart from projection and denial, for dealing with his suffering—he could make films. It is conceivable that we, as the movie audience, have to endure those feelings that he, the son of such a father, could not experience overtly but nevertheless carried within himself. We sit before the screen confronted, the way that small boy once was, with all the cruelty 'our brother' has to endure, and hardly feel able or willing to take in all this brutality with authentic feelings; we ward them off. When Bergman speaks regretfully of his failure to see through Nazism before 1945, although as an adolescent he often visited Germany during the Hitler period, we may see it as a consequence of his childhood. Cruelty was the familiar air that he had breathed from early on—and so, why should cruelty have caught his attention?

And why did I describe these three examples of men who had been beaten in their childhood? Are these not borderline cases? Do I want to consider the effects of beatings? By no means. We may believe that these three cases are crass exceptions. However, I chose these examples partly because they had not been entrusted to me as secrets but had already been made public, but, above all, I meant to show how even the most severe ill-treatment can remain hidden, because of the child's strong tendency to idealization. There is no trial, no advocate, no verdict; everything remains hidden in the darkness of the past, and should the facts become known, then they appear in the name of blessings. If this is so with the crassest examples of physical ill-treatment, then how is mental torment ever to be exposed, when it is less visible and more easily disputed anyway? Who is likely to take serious notice of subtle discrimination, as in the example of the small boy and the ice cream?

Metapsychology has no model for these processes. It is concerned with cathexis, with intrapsychic dynamics, object- and self-representations, but not with facts that at most are taken into account as the patient's fantasies. Its concern is the meaning attached to experiences and not the reality behind them. Nevertheless, we do analyse parents, too, and we hear about their feelings towards their children and about their narcissistic needs, and we have to ask ourselves what the consequences of all this are for the development of their children. What are we to do with this information? Can we ignore its implications? Can we blind ourselves with the argument that an analyst is only concerned with intrapsychic processes? It is as if we did not dare to take a single step in order to acknowledge the child's reality, since Freud recognized the conjecture of sexual seduction as the patient's fantasy. Since the patient also has an interest in keeping this reality hidden from us, and still more from himself, it can happen that we share his ignorance for a long time. Nevertheless, the patient never stops telling us about part of his reality in the language of his symptoms.

Possibly, the child's actual seduction did not take place the way Freud's hysterical patients related it. Yet, the parents' narcissistic cathexis of their child leads to a long series of sexual and nonsexual seductions, which the child will only be able to discover with difficulty, as an adult in his analysis (and often not before he himself is a parent).

A father who grew up in surroundings inimical to instinctual drives may well be inhibited in his sexual relationships in marriage. He may even remain polymorphous perverse and first dare to look properly at a female genital, play with it, and feel aroused while he is bathing his small daughter. A mother may perhaps have been shocked as a small girl by the unexpected sight of an erect penis and so developed fear of the male genital, or she may have experienced it as a symbol of violence in the primal scene without being able to confide in anyone. Such a mother may now be able to gain control over her fear in relationship to her tiny son. She may, for example, dry him after his bath in such a manner that he has an erection, which is not dangerous or threatening for her. She may massage her son's penis, right up to puberty, in order 'to treat his phimosis' without having to be afraid. Protected by the unquestioning love that every child has for his mother she can carry on with her genuine, hesitating sexual exploration that had been broken off too soon.

What does it mean to the child, though, when his sexually inhibited parents make narcissistic use of him in their loneliness and need? Every child seeks loving contact and is happy to get it. At the same time, however, he feels insecure when desires are aroused that do not appear spontaneously at this stage in his development. This insecurity is further increased by the fact that his own autoerotic activity is punished by the parents' prohibitions or scorn.

There are other ways of seducing the child, apart from the sexual, for instance, with the aid of indoctrination, which underlies both the 'anti-authoritarian' and the 'strict' upbringing. Neither form of rearing takes account of the child's needs at his particular stage of development. As soon as the child is regarded as a possession for which one has a particular goal, as soon as one exerts control over him, his vital growth will be violently interrupted.

It is among the commonplaces of education that we often first cut off the living root and then try to replace its natural functions by artificial means. Thus we suppress the child's curiosity, for example (there are questions one should not ask), and then when he lacks a natural interest in learning he is offered special coaching for his scholastic difficulties.

We find a similar example in the behaviour of addicts, in whom the object relationship has already been internalized. People who as children successfully repressed their intense feelings often try to regain—at least for a short time—their lost intensity of experience with the help of drugs or alcohol.

If we want to avoid the unconscious seduction and discrimination against the child, we must first gain a conscious awareness of these dangers. Only if we become sensitive to the fine and subtle ways in which a child may suffer humiliation can we hope to develop the respect for him that a child needs from the very first day of his life onward, if he is to develop emotionally. There are various ways to reach this sensitivity. We may, for instance, observe children who are strangers to us and attempt to feel empathy for them in their situation—or we might try to develop empathy for our own fate. For us as analysts, there is also the possibility of following our analysand into his past—if we accept that his feelings will tell us a true story that so far no one else knows.

The Vicious Circle of Contempt

INTROJECTED CONTEMPT IN THE MIRROR OF PSYCHOANALYSIS

DAMAGED SELF-ARTICULATION IN THE COMPULSION TO REPEAT

If we want to do more than provide patients with intellectual insight, or—as may be necessary in some psychotherapies—merely to strengthen their defence mechanisms, then we shall have to embark on a new voyage of discovery with each patient. What we so discover will not be a distant land but one that does not yet exist and will only begin to do so in the course of its discovery and settlement. It is a fascinating experience to accompany a patient on this journey—so long as we do not try to enter this new land with concepts that are familiar to us, perhaps in order to avoid our own fear of what is unknown and not yet understood. The patient discovers his true self little by little through experiencing his own feelings and needs, because the analyst is able to accept and respect these even when he does not yet understand them.

I am sometimes asked in seminars or supervisor's sessions how one should deal with 'undesirable' feelings such as the irritation that patients sometimes arouse in their analyst. A sensitive analyst will, of course, feel this irritation. Should he suppress it to avoid rejecting the patient? But then the patient, too, will sense this suppressed anger, without being able to comprehend it, and will be confused. Should the analyst express it? If he does, this may offend the patient and undermine his confidence. I have found that when I do not attempt to respond to such questions and remarks with advice, the discussion among colleagues reaches a much deeper and more personal dimension. The question of how to deal with anger and other feelings in the countertransference no longer needs to be asked if we begin with the assumption that *all* the feelings that the patient arouses in his analyst, during his analysis, are part of his unconscious attempt to tell the analyst his story and at the same time to hide it from him—that is, to protect himself from the renewed manipulation he unconsciously expects. I always assume that the patient has no other way of telling me his story than the one he actually uses. Seen thus, all feelings arising in me, including irritation, belong to his coded language and are of great heuristic value. At times they may help to find the lost key to still invisible doors.

At one time there was discussion in the literature about how to recognize whether countertransference feelings are an expression of the analyst's transference. If the analyst has gained emotional access to his own childhood, then he should easily be able to distinguish between countertransference feelings and his own childish ones (his own transference). Feelings that belong to the countertransference are like a quick flash, a signal, and clearly related to the analysand's person. When they are intense, tormenting, and continuous, they have to do with oneself. The countertransference indicates either the former attitudes of the patient's primary objects (or the analyst's unconscious rejection of this role), or the child's feelings, split-off and never experienced, which the patient in the course of his analysis has delegated to his analyst.

Can one portray a story that one does not know? This sounds impossible—but it happens in every analysis. The patient needs the analytic situation as a framework for the development of his transference before he can stage his story and make it understood. He needs somebody who does not need him to behave in a particular manner, but can let him be as he is at the moment, and who at the same time is willing to accept any of the roles with which he may be charged for as long as the analytic process requires.

The compulsion to repeat plays a prominent role in an analysis conceived in this way. Much has been written about the negative aspect of the compulsion to repeat: the uncanny tendency to re-enact a trauma, which itself is not remembered, at times has something cruel and self-destructive about it and understandably suggests associations with the death instinct. Nevertheless, the need to repeat also has a positive side. Repetition is the language used by a child who has remained dumb, his only means of expressing himself. A dumb child needs a particularly emphatic partner if he is to be understood at all. Speech, on the other hand, is often used less to express genuine feelings and thoughts than to hide, veil or deny them, and thus to express the false self. And so there often are long periods in our work with our patients during which we are dependent on their compulsion to repeat—for this repetition is then the only manifestation of their true self. It lays the basis for the transference, and also for the whole mise en scène of the patient's field of interaction, which in the literature is described as acting out and is often met with mistrust.

Take an example. In many analyses the patient's wish to have a child is expressed during the first weeks or months. For a long time this wish was traced back to Oedipal wishes. This may well be correct. Nevertheless, the patient's associations often show the narcissistic background to this wish very clearly.

For the patient this means: 'I want to have somebody whom I can completely possess, and whom I can control (my mother always withdrew from me); somebody who will stay with me all the time and not only for four hours in the week. Right now I am nobody, but as a mother or a father I should be somebody, and others would value me more than they do now that I have no children.' Or it may mean: 'I want to give a child everything that I had to do without, he should be free, not have to deny himself, be able to develop freely. I want to give this chance to another human being.'

This second variation looks as though it were based on object relationships. But if that were so the patient would be able to take his time in fulfilling this wish—and to wait until he would be able to give from his abundance towards the end of his analysis. If, however, this wish for a child at the beginning of the analysis cannot be delayed but shows such urgency, then it is rather an expression of the patient's own great need.

Various aspects come together:

- The wish to have a mother who is available (the child as a new chance to achieve the good symbiosis, which

the patient still seeks since he has never experienced
it).

- The hope that with this birth the patient may become
truly alive (the child as symbol for the patient's true
self).

- Unconscious communication about the patient's own
fate as a child, with the aid of compulsive repetition
(the child as rival sibling, and abandoned hope); the
sibling's birth had increased the patient's loss of self,
and with the birth of his child the patient would give
up (for the time being) his hope of realizing his true
self.

To interpret this questionable wish to have a child as
acting-out is not usually successful, since the compulsion to repeat is too strong. The analyst is then
experienced as a strict mother, against whom the
patient would like to rebel. At present, however, the
patient can do so only in this self-destructive way, since
he is not yet free from introjects. So the analyst is forced
to be a spectator while the patient gives life to a new
human being, apparently in order to destroy his own
chance, but also thereby to rediscover his formerly only
half-experienced life and to experience it consciously
now with his newly awakened feelings. Just as a child
uses the Sceno test figures to represent his family, so the
patient unconsciously uses his newborn child to lay out
for himself the tragedy of his own fate.

This is the double function of the compulsion to
repeat. The patient senses that here for the first time he
is really involved, that it is his own self that is being
born. The wish to have a child expresses this desire, but
it has to be expressed through another person. For the

patient now will devote himself not to the baby he once was, but to an actual baby in the present. However, since this newborn baby also stands for his own childhood self, the patient can emotionally discover his own warded-off childhood story, piece by piece, partly through identification and partly in the guise of his own parents, whom he gradually discovers within himself.

The compulsion to repeat is, in fact, more or less powerful even outside analysis. It is, for example, well-known that partner choice is closely related to the primary object's character. In analysis, however, this tendency is particularly strong—above all because the staging here includes the analyst, and the patient feels that a solution can be found. A detour by way of secondary transference figures is nevertheless often unavoidable, since fear of object-loss becomes intolerable as soon as ambivalent feelings develop. It is still necessary to separate the 'mother as environment' from the 'mother as object'. The patient has learned very early in life that he must not show any dissatisfaction or disappointment with the object, since this would lead to the beloved father or mother withdrawing himself and his love. In the analysis a stage must certainly be reached, when even this risk can be endured and survived. Before that time, however, there is a long period when the analyst is needed as a companion, while early experiences with the primary objects which hitherto were inaccessible to memory, are rediscovered in a trial run with secondary transference figures.

The newly won capacity to accept his feelings frees the way for the patient's long-repressed needs and wishes, which nevertheless cannot yet be satisfied without self-punishment, or even cannot in reality be satisfied at all, since they are related to past situations. The latter is clearly seen in the example of the urgent and not to be postponed wish for a child, which, as I have tried to describe, expresses among other things the wish to have a mother constantly available.

All the same, there are needs that can and should be satisfied in the present and that regularly come up in the analyses of narcissistically disturbed individuals. Among these is every human being's central need to express himself—to show himself to the world as he really is—in word, in gesture, in behaviour, in every genuine utterance from the baby's cry to the artist's creation.

For those people who, as children, had to hide their true selves from themselves and others, this first step into the open produces much anxiety. Yet, these people, especially, feel a great need to throw over their former restraints within the protection of their analysis. These first steps do not lead to freedom but to a compulsive repetition of the patient's childhood constellation, and so he will experience those feelings of agonizing shame and painful nakedness that accompany self-display. With the infallibility of a sleepwalker, the analysand seeks out those who, like his parents (though for different reasons), certainly cannot understand him. Through his compulsive need to repeat, he will try to make himself understandable to precisely these people—trying to make possible what cannot be.

At a particular stage in her analysis, a young woman

fell in love with an older, intelligent and sensitive man, who nevertheless, apart from eroticism, had to ward off and reject everything he could not understand intellectually, including psychoanalysis. Precisely this person was the one to whom she wrote long letters trying to explain the path she had taken in her analysis up to this point. She succeeded in overlooking all his signals of incomprehension and increased her efforts even more, until at last she was forced to recognize that she had again found a father substitute, and that this was the reason why she had been unable to give up her hopes of at last being understood. This awakening brought her agonizingly sharp feelings of shame that lasted for a long time. One day she was able to experience this during a session and said: 'I feel so ridiculous, as if I had been talking to a wall and expecting it to answer, like a silly child.' I asked: 'Would you think it ridiculous if you saw a child who had to tell his troubles to a wall because there was no one else available?' The despairing sobbing that followed my question gave the patient access to a part of her former reality that was pervaded by boundless loneliness. It freed her at the same time from her agonizing, destructive, and compulsively repeated feelings of shame. The following day this patient brought her first poem, which she had written that night.

Only much later could she risk repeating this experience with 'a wall' with me and not only with subsidiary transference figures. For a time this woman, who was normally capable of expressing herself so clearly, described everything in such an extraordinarily complicated and precipitate way that I had no chance of understanding it all, probably much like her parents earlier. She went through moments of sudden hate and narcissistic rage, reproaching me with indifference and lack of understanding. My patient now could hardly recognize me any more, although I had not changed. In this way she rediscovered with me her own childhood. A child, too, can never grasp the fact that the same mother who cooks so well, is so concerned about his cough, and helps so kindly with his homework, in some circumstances has no more feeling than a wall for his hidden inner world. This young woman's vehement reproaches that now were directed against me finally released her from her compulsion to repeat, which had consisted of constantly seeking a partner who had no understanding for her or of arranging such a constellation, so that she would then feel helplessly dependent on him. The fascination of such tormenting relationships is part of the compulsion constantly to re-enact one's earliest disappointments with the parents.

PERPETUATION OF CONTEMPT IN PERVERSION AND OBSESSIONAL NEUROSIS

If we start from the premise that a person's whole development (and his narcissistic balance that is based upon it) is dependent on the way *his mother* experienced his *expression of needs and sensations* during his first days and weeks of life, then we must assume that here the *valuation* of *feelings* and *impulses* is set. If a mother cannot take pleasure in her child as he is but must have

him behave in a particular way, then the first value
selection takes place for the child. Now 'good' is
differentiated from 'bad', 'nice' from 'nasty', and 'right'
from 'wrong', and this differentiation is introjected by
the child. Against this background will follow all his
further introjections of the parents' more differentiated
valuations.

Since every mother has her own 'roomful of props',
virtually every infant must learn that there are things
about him for which the mother has 'no use'. She will
expect her child to control his bodily functions as early
as possible. On the conscious level his parents want him
to do this so that he will not offend against society, but
unconsciously they are protecting their own reaction
formation dating from the time when they were
themselves small children afraid of 'offending'.

Marie Hesse, the mother of the poet and novelist
Hermann Hesse, undoubtedly a sensitive woman,
describes in her diaries how her own will was broken at
the age of four. When her son was four years old, she
suffered greatly under his defiant behaviour, and
battled against it with varying degrees of success. At
the age of fifteen, Hermann Hesse was sent to an
institution for the care of epileptics and defectives in
Stetten, 'to put an end to his defiance once and for all'. In
an affecting and angry letter from Stetten, Hesse wrote
to his parents: 'If I were a bigot, and not a human being,
I could perhaps hope for your understanding.' All the
same, his release from the home was made conditional
upon his 'improvement', and so the boy 'improved'. In a
later poem dedicated to his parents, denial and idealiza-

tion are restored: he reproaches himself that it had been 'his character' that had made life so difficult for his parents. Many people suffer all their lives from this oppressive feeling of guilt, the sense of not having lived up to their parents' expectations. This feeling is stronger than any intellectual insight that it is not a child's task or duty to satisfy his parents' narcissistic needs. No argument can overcome these guilt feelings, for they have their beginnings in life's earliest period, and from that they derive their intensity and obduracy.

That probably greatest of narcissistic wounds—not to have been loved just as one truly was—cannot heal without the work of mourning. It can either be more or less successfully resisted and covered up (as in grandiosity and depression), or constantly torn open again in the compulsion to repeat. We encounter this last possibility in obsessional neurosis and in perversion. The mother's (or father's) scornful reactions have been introjected. The mother often reacted with surprise and horror, aversion and disgust, shock and indignation, or with fear and panic to the child's most natural impulses. And so these have been the mother's reactions to such natural impulses as the child's autoerotic behaviour, investigating and discovering his own body, oral greed, urination and defecation, touching and playing with his own excrement, or to his curiosity or rage in response to failure or disappointment. Later, all these experiences remain closely linked to the mother's horrified eyes, and this clearly emerges in the analytic transference.

The patient goes through torment when he reveals to the analyst his hitherto secret sexual and autoerotic behaviour. He may, of course, also relate all this quite unemotionally, merely giving information, as if he were speaking of some other person. Such a report, however, will not help him to break out of his loneliness nor lead him back to the reality of his childhood. It is only when he is encouraged in the analysis not to fend off his feelings of shame and fear, but rather to accept and experience them, that he can discover what he has felt as a child. His most harmless behaviour will cause him to feel mean, dirty, or completely annihilated. He himself indeed is surprised when he realizes how long this repressed feeling of shame has survived, and how it has found a place alongside his tolerant and advanced views of sexuality. These experiences first show the patient that his early adaptation by means of splitting was not an expression of cowardice, but that it was really his only chance to escape this sense of impending destruction.

What else can one expect of a mother who was always proud of being her mother's dear good daughter, who was dry at the age of six months, clean at a year, at three could 'mother' her younger siblings, and so forth. In her own baby, such a mother sees the split-off and never-experienced part of her self, of whose breakthrough into consciousness she is afraid, and she sees also the uninhibited sibling baby, whom she mothered at such an early age and only now envies and perhaps hates in the person of her own child. So she trains her child with looks, despite her greater wisdom—for she can do nothing else. As the child grows up, he cannot cease living his own truth, and expressing it somewhere, perhaps in complete secrecy. In this way a person can have adapted completely to the demands of his surroundings and can have developed a false self, but in his perversion or his obsessional neurosis he still allows a portion of his true self to survive—in torment. And so the true self lives on, under the same conditions as the child once did with his disgusted mother, whom in the meantime he has introjected. In his perversion and obsessions he constantly re-enacts the same drama: a horrified mother is necessary before drive-satisfaction is possible; orgasm (for instance, with a fetish) can only be achieved in a climate of self-contempt; criticism can only be expressed in (seemingly) absurd, unaccountable (frightening), obsessional fantasies.

Nothing will serve better to acquaint us with the hidden tragedy of certain unconscious mother-child relationships than the analysis of a perversion or an obsessional neurosis. For in such an analysis we witness the destructive power of the compulsion to repeat, and that compulsion's dumb, unconscious communication in the shaping of its drama.

It is of eminent importance that, although the patient has the possibility to *experience* the analyst as hostile to his drives, critical and contemptuous, yet the analyst should, in fact, never really be so. This may sound obvious but it is not always in practice.

Sometimes the analyst does just the opposite, quite unconsciously and with the best intentions. It may be that he can hardly bear being turned into a figure so hostile to instinctual drives, and so must demonstrate his tolerance by persuading the patient, for example, to describe his masturbatory practice fearlessly. In doing so he will prevent the patient from experiencing his mother in the transference. At the same time this analyst repeats, in reality, the mother's rejection of the patient's childish instinctual impulses, for he does not allow the childish fear and confusion to come out as they were originally felt and will only speak to his patient on an adult level.

One might, in fact, think of it as discrimination, as a devaluation of the childlike, when an analyst emphasizes that, for him, of course, his patients are always adults and not children—as if being a child were something to be ashamed of, and not something valuable that we lose later on. Occasionally one hears similar remarks about sickness, when an analyst is eager to consider his patients as healthy as possible, or warns them against 'dangerous regression'—as if sickness were not sometimes the only possible way of expressing the true self. The people who come to us have, after all, been trying all their lives to be as adult and healthy (normal) as possible. They experience it as a great, inner liberation when they discover this socially conditioned straitjacket of child-rejection and 'normalcy'-worship within themselves and can give it up.

A person who suffers under his perversion bears within himself his mother's rejection, and thus he flaunts his perversion, in order to get others to reject him, too, all the time—so re-externalizing the rejecting mother. For this reason he feels compelled to do things that his circle and society disapprove of and despise. If society were suddenly to honour his form of perversion (as may happen in certain circles), he would have to change his compulsion, but it would not free him. What he needs is not permission to use one or another fetish, but the disgusted and horrified eyes. If he comes to analysis he will look for this in his analyst, too, and will have to use all possible means to provoke him to disgust, horror and aversion. This provocation is of course a part of the transference, and from the incipient counter-transference reactions one can surmise what happened at the beginning of this life.

If the analyst can see through to the goals and compulsions behind this provocation, then the whole decayed building collapses and gives way to true, deep, and defenceless mourning. When finally the narcissistic wound itself can be felt, there is no more necessity for all the distortions. This is a clear demonstration of how mistaken the attempt is to show a patient his instinctual conflicts, if he has been trained from earliest childhood on to *feel nothing*. How can instinctual wishes and conflicts be experienced without feelings? What can orality mean without greed, what anality without defiance and envy, what is the Oedipus complex without feelings of rage, abandonment, jealousy, loneliness, love? It is very striking to see how often pseudoinstinctual acting-out ceases when the patient begins to experience *his own* feelings and can recognize his *true* instinctual wishes.

The following citation is taken from a report about St Pauli, Hamburg's red-light district, that appeared in the German magazine *Stern* (8 June 1978): 'You experience the masculine dream, as seductive as it is absurd, of being coddled by women like a baby and at the same time commanding them like a pascha.' This 'masculine dream', indeed is not absurd; it arises from the infant's most genuine and legitimate needs. Our world would be very different if the majority of babies had the chance to rule over their mothers like paschas and to be coddled by them, without having to concern themselves with their mothers' needs too early.

The reporter asked some of the regular clients what gave them most pleasure in these establishments and summarized their answers as follows:

> . . . that the girls are available and completely at the customer's disposal, they do *not require protestations of love like girlfriends.* There are *no obligations, psychological dramas,* nor *pangs of conscience* when desire has passed: '*You pay and are free!*' Even (and especially) the *humiliation* that such an encounter also involves for the client can *increase stimulation—* but that is less willingly mentioned [my italics].

The humiliation, self-disgust, and self-contempt are intrapsychic reflections of the primary objects' contempt and, through the compulsion to repeat, they produce the same tragic conditions for pleasure.

Perversion is a borderline case, but gives us an understanding that is valid for the treatment of other disorders, namely, understanding of the great importance to be attached to unconscious, introjected contempt.

What is unconscious cannot be abolished by proclamation or prohibition. One can, however, develop sensitivity toward recognizing it and can experience it consciously, and thus gain control over it. A mother can have the best intentions to respect her child and yet be unable to do so, so long as she does not realize what deep shame she causes him with an ironic remark, intended only to cover her own uncertainty. Indeed, she cannot be aware of how deeply humiliated, despised, and devalued her child feels, if she herself has never consciously suffered these feelings, and if she tries to fend them off with irony.

It can be the same for us in our analytic work. Certainly, we do not use words like bad, dirty, naughty, egoistic, rotten—but among ourselves we speak of 'narcissistic', 'exhibitionistic', 'destructive' and 'regressive' patients, without noticing that we (unconsciously) give these words a pejorative meaning. It may be that in our abstract vocabulary, in our objective attitudes, even in the way we formulate our theories, we have something in common with a mother's contemptuous looks, which we can trace to the accommodating three-year-old little girl within her. It is understandable that a patient's scornful attitude should induce an analyst to protect his superiority with the help of theory. But in such a dugout the patient's true self will not pay us a visit. It will hide from us just as it did from the mother's disgusted eyes. However, we make good use of our sensitivity. We can detect the successive instalments in the story of a despised child, that lies behind all the analysand's expressions of contempt. When that happens, it is easier for the analyst not to feel he is being attacked and to drop his inner need to hide behind his theories. The knowledge of theory is surely helpful, but only when it has lost its defensive function—when it no longer is the successor of a strict, controlling mother, forcing the analyst to accommodate himself, and narrowing his possibilities. Then the knowledge of theory is like Winnicott's 'teddy bear, lying about'—simply within reach when it is needed.

'DEPRAVITY' IN HERMANN HESSE'S CHILDHOOD
WORLD AS AN EXAMPLE OF CONCRETE 'EVIL'

It is very difficult to describe how a person has dealt with the contempt under which he had suffered as a child—especially the contempt for all his sensual enjoyment and pleasure in living—without giving concrete examples. With the aid of various metapsychological models one could certainly portray the intrapsychic dynamics, shifts in cathexis, structural changes and various defence mechanisms, especially the defence against effect. None of this, however, would communicate the emotional climate, which alone evokes a person's suffering, and so will make identification and empathy possible for the reader. With purely theoretical representations we remain 'outside', can talk about 'the others', classify, group, and label them, and discuss them in a language that only we understand.

There is, of course, an inequality in the analytic setting (between the analysand on his couch and the analyst in his chair), which has both point and validity. But there is no essential reason to extend it to other situations, such as discussions, lectures and articles. Thus I must reduce the inequality and distance between couch and chair in myself, if I want to avoid degrading patients to scientific specimens for my study.

How is this to be put into practice if one feels called upon not only to accompany the patient but also to pass on the experience one has gained? Metapsychological concepts alone do not make it clear how far we all as human beings (as small children and as analysands) have need of our common sensitivity. If, however, I describe examples in detail, then I am in danger of revealing a person's secret and hidden tragedy to the world. I thereby should (in effect though not by intention) be repeating the mother's lack of respect, for instance, when she discovered the child's masturbation and shamed him for it. Yet, it is only through the concrete example of a specific life that we can show how a person has experienced the concrete 'naughtiness' of his childhood as 'wickedness itself'. Only the history of an individual life will make us realize how impossible it is for an individual to recognize his parents' compulsion as such, once they have become part of himself— although he may try all his life to break out of this inner prison.

In this dilemma between metapsychology and indiscretion I have decided to use the example of the poet and novelist Hermann Hesse to demonstrate the very complicated situation. This eliminates from the beginning any moral evaluation, and although it does not concern a perversion, it does seem to me to have something in common with the early history of a perversion, namely, the introjection of parental contempt for the child's instinctual needs. This example also has the advantage that it has been published, and published by the person himself, so that the connections that I shall postulate can be clarified with concrete examples from his life.

At the beginning of his novel *Demian*, Hermann Hesse describes the goodness and purity of a parental home that gave neither a place nor a hearing to a child's fibs. (It is not difficult to recognize the author's own parental home in this novel, and he confirms this indirectly.) Thus the child is left alone with his sin and feels that he is depraved, wicked, and outcast, though nobody scolds him (since nobody knows the 'terrible facts') and everyone shows him kindness and friendliness.

Many people recognize this situation. The idealizing way of describing such a 'pure' household is not strange to us either, and it reflects both the child's point of view and the hidden cruelty of educational methods that we know well.

> Like most parents [writes Hesse], mine were no help with the new problems of puberty, to which no reference was ever made. All they did was take *endless trouble* in supporting my hopeless attempts to *deny reality* and to continue dwelling in a childhood world that was becoming *more and more unreal*. I have no idea whether parents can be of help, and I do not blame mine. It was my own affair to come to terms with myself and to find my own way, and like most well-brought-up children, I managed it badly [my italics]. (p. 49)

The Vicious Circle of Contempt

To a child his parents seem to be free of instinctual wishes, for they have means and possibilities of hiding their sexual satisfactions, whereas the child is always under surveillance.*

The first part of *Demian*, it seems to me, is very evocative and easy to appreciate, even for people from quite different milieu. What makes the later parts of the novel so peculiarly difficult must be in some way related to Hesse's introjection of his parents' and grandparents' emotional values (they were missionary families), which is to be felt in many of his stories, but can perhaps most easily be shown in *Demian*.

Although Sinclair has already had his own experience of cruelty (blackmail by an older boy), this has had no effect and gives him no key to a better understanding of the world. 'Wickedness' for him is 'depravity' (here is the missionaries' language). It is neither the hate, nor the ambivalence, nor the cruelty that are present in every human being and that Sinclair himself has already experienced, but such trivialities as drinking in a tavern.

The little boy Hermann Hesse took over from his parents this particular concept of wickedness as 'depravity': it is not rooted in his personality but is like a foreign body. This is why everything in *Demian* that

* In his story 'A Child's Heart' Hesse writes: 'The adults acted as if the world were perfect and as if they themselves were demigods, we children were nothing but scum. . . . Again and again, after a few days, even after a few hours, something happened that should not have been allowed, something wretched, depressing, and shaming. Again and again, in the midst of the noblest and staunchest decisions and vows, I fell abruptly, inescapably, into sin and wickedness, into ordinary bad habits. Why was it this way?' (pp. 7, 8)

happens after the appearance of the god Abraxas, who is to 'unite the godly and the devilish', is so curiously removed, it no longer touches us. Wickedness here is supposed to be artfully united with goodness. One has the impression that, for the boy, this is something strange, threatening, and above all unknown, from which he nevertheless cannot free himself, because of his emotional cathexis of 'depravity', which is already joined to fear and guilt. 'Once more I was trying most strenuously to construct an intimate "world of light" for myself out of the shambles of a period of devastation; once more I sacrificed everything within me to the aim of banishing darkness and evil from myself.' (pp. 81–2)

In the Zürich exhibition (1977) to commemorate the centenary of Hesse's birth, there was a picture with which the little Hermann grew up, since it hung above his bed. In this picture, on the right, we see the 'good' road to heaven, full of thorns, difficulties, and suffering. On the left, we see the easy pleasurable road that inevitably leads to hell. Taverns play a prominent part on this road—the devout women probably hoped to keep their husbands and sons away from these wicked places with this threatening representation. These taverns play an important role in *Demian*, too. This is particularly grotesque because Hesse had no urge at all to get drunk in such taverns, though he certainly did wish to break out of the narrowness of his parental system of values.

Every child forms his first image of what is 'bad', quite concretely, by what is forbidden—by his parents' prohibitions, taboos and fears. He will have a long way to go until he can free himself from these parental values and discover his own 'badness' in himself. He then will no longer regard it as 'depraved' and 'wicked', because it is instinctual, but as an aspect of life from which no human being can be free at bottom—although the strength of their disavowal may be sufficient for some people to convince themselves that they are. Possibly, Hermann Hesse in his puberty also had to live out his father's split-off and denied 'depravity', and this he tried to portray in his books. Perhaps this is why there is so much in his novels that is not easy to empathize with, though it communicates the atmosphere under which Hesse suffered as a child, and from which he could not free himself, because he had been compelled to introject it so very early.

The following passage from *Demian* shows how deeply the loss of the loved objects threatened Hesse's search for his true self:

> But where we have given of our love and respect not from habit but of our own free will, where we have been disciples and friends out of our inmost hearts, it is a bitter and horrible moment when we suddenly recognize that the current within us wants to pull us away from what is dearest to us. Then every thought that rejects the friend and mentor turns in our own hearts like *a poisoned barb*, then each blow struck in defense *flies back into one's own face*, the words 'disloyalty' and 'ingratitude' strike the person who feels he was morally sound *like catcalls and stigma*, and the *frightened heart flees timidly back* to the *charmed valleys of childhood* virtues, unable to believe that this break, too, must be made, this bond also broken [my italics]. (p. 127)

The Vicious Circle of Contempt

And in 'A Child's Heart' we read:

> If I were to reduce all my feelings and their painful
> conflicts to a single name, I can think of no other word
> but: dread. It was dread, dread and uncertainty, that I
> felt in all those hours of shattered childhood felicity:
> dread of punishment, dread of my own conscience,
> dread of stirrings in my soul which I considered
> forbidden and criminal. (p. 10)

In his story 'A Child's Heart' Hesse portrays with
great tenderness and understanding the feelings of an
eleven-year-old boy, who had stolen some dried figs
from his beloved father's room so that he could have in
his possession something that belonged to his father.
Guilt feelings, fear, and despair torment him in his
loneliness and are replaced at last by the deepest
humiliation and shame when his 'wicked deed' is
discovered. The strength of this portrayal leads us to
surmise that it concerns a real episode from Hesse's own
childhood. This surmise becomes certainty, thanks to a
note made by his mother on 11 November 1889:
'Hermann's theft of figs discovered.'

From the entries in his mother's diary and from the
extensive exchange of letters between both parents and
various members of the family, which have been
available since 1966, it is possible to guess at the small
boy's painful path. Hesse, like so many gifted children,
was so difficult for his parents to bear, not despite but
because of his inner riches. Often a child's very gifts, his
great intensity of feeling, depth of experience, curiosity,
intelligence, quickness—and his ability to be critical—

will confront his parents with conflicts that they have long sought to keep at bay with rules and regulations. These regulations must then be rescued at the cost of the child's development. All this can lead to the apparently paradoxical situation when parents who are proud of their gifted child and who even admire him are forced by their own distress to reject, suppress, or even destroy what is *best*, because truest, in that child. Two of Hesse's mother's observations may illustrate how this work of destruction can be combined with loving care:

(1881) Hermann is going to nursery school, his violent temperament causes us much distress. [The child was three years old.]

(1884) Things are going better with Hermann, whose education causes us so much distress and trouble. From the 21st of January to the 5th of June he lived wholly in the boys' house and only spent Sundays with us. He behaved well there but came home pale, thin and *depressed*. The *effects are decidedly good and salutary*. He is much *easier to manage now*. [My italics. The child now was seven years old.] (1966, pp. 10 and 13–14)

On 14 November 1883, his father, Johannes Hesse, writes:

Hermann, who was considered almost a model of good behavior in the boys' house is sometimes *hardly to be borne*. Though it would be very humiliating *for us* [!], I am earnestly considering whether we should not place him in an *institution* or *another household*. We are too nervous and weak for him, and the whole household [is] too undisciplined and irregular. He seems to be gifted for everything: he observes the moon and the clouds, extemporizes for long periods on the harmonium, draws wonderful pictures with pencil or pen, can sing quite well when he wants to, and is never at a loss for a rhyme [my italics]. (1966, p. 13)

In the strongly idealized picture of his childhood and his parents, which we encounter in *Hermann Lauscher*,* Hesse has completely abandoned the original, rebellious, 'difficult', and for his parents troublesome, child he once was. He had no way to accommodate this important part of his self and so was forced to expel it. Perhaps this is why his great and genuine longing for his true self remained unfulfilled.

That Hermann Hesse was not deficient in courage, talent, or depth of feeling is, of course, evident in his works and in many of his letters, especially the unforgettable letter from Stetten. But his father's answer to this letter (cf. 1966), his mother's notes, and the passages from *Demian* and 'Kinderseele' quoted above show us clearly how the crushing weight of his introjects became his fate. Despite his enormous acclaim

---

* 'When my childhood at times stirs my heart, it is like a gold-framed, deep-toned picture in which predominates a wealth of chestnuts and alders, an indescribably delightful morning light and a background of splendid mountains. All the hours in my life, in which I was allowed a short period of peace, forgetful of the world; all the lonely walks, which I took over beautiful mountains; all the moments in which an unexpected happiness, or love without desire, carried me away from yesterday and tomorrow; all these can be given no more precious name than when I compare them with this green picture of my earliest life.' (*Gesammelte Werke*, vol. I, 1970, p. 218)

and success, and despite the Nobel prize, Hesse in his mature years suffered from the tragic and painful feeling of being separated from his true self, which doctors refer to curtly as depression.

THE MOTHER DURING THE FIRST YEARS OF LIFE AS SOCIETY'S AGENT*

If we were to tell a patient that in other societies his perversion would not be a problem, that it is a problem here sheerly because it is our society that is sick and produces constrictions and constraints, this would certainly be partially true, but it would be of little help to him. He would feel, rather, that, as an individual, with his own individual history, he was being passed over and misunderstood; for this interpretation makes too little of his own very real tragedy. What most needs to be understood is his compulsion to repeat, and the state of affairs behind it to which this compulsion bears witness. All this no doubt is the result of social pressures, and these do not have their effect on his psyche through abstract knowledge but are anchored in his earliest affective experience with his mother. His problems cannot be solved with *words*, but only through *experience*, not merely corrective experience as an adult but, above all, through a reliving of his early fear of his beloved mother's contempt and his subsequent feelings of indignation and sadness. Mere words, however skilled the interpretation, will leave the split from which he suffers unchanged or even deepened.

* See footnote on p. 22.

One can therefore hardly free a patient from the cruelty of his introjects by showing him how the absurdity, exploitation and perversity of society causes our neuroses and perversions, however true this may be. Freud's patient Dora became sick because of society's sexual hypocrisy, which she was unable to see through. Things we can see through do not make us sick; they may arouse our indignation, anger, sadness or feelings of impotence. What makes us sick are those things we cannot see through, society's constraints that we have absorbed through our mother's eyes—eyes and an attitude from which no reading or learning can free us. To put it another way: our patients are intelligent, they read in newspapers and books about the absurdity of the armaments race, about exploitation through capitalism, diplomatic insincerity, the arrogance and manipulation of power, submission of the weak and the impotence of individuals—and they have thought about these subjects. What they do not see, because they cannot see it, is the absurdities of their own mothers at the time when they still were tiny children. One cannot remember one's parents' attitudes then, because one was a part of them, but in analysis this early interaction can be recalled and parental constraints are thus more easily disclosed.

Political action can be fed by the unconscious anger of children who have been so misused, imprisoned, exploited, cramped and drilled. This anger can be partially discharged in fighting our institutions, without having to give up the idealization of one's own mother, as one knew her in one's childhood. The old dependency can then be shifted to a new object. If, however, disillusionment and the resultant mourning can be lived through in analysis, then social and political disengagement do not usually follow, but the patient's actions are freed from the compulsion to repeat.

The inner necessity to constantly build up new illusions and denials, in order to avoid the experience of our own reality, disappears once this reality has been faced and experienced. We then realize that all our lives we have feared and struggled to ward off something that really cannot happen any longer: it has already happened, happened at the very beginning of our lives while we were completely dependent. The situation is similar in regard to creativity. Here the prerequisite is the work of mourning—not a neurosis, although people often think it is the latter—and many artists believe that analysis (the mother?) would 'take away' their creativity.

Let us assume that an analyst tries to talk a patient out of his guilt feelings by tracing his strict superego back to those of society's norms that serve particular capitalist interests. This interpretation is not false. 'Society' not only suppresses instinctual wishes but also (and above all) it suppresses particular feelings (for instance, anger) and narcissistic needs (for esteem, mirroring, respect), whose admissibility in adults and fulfilment in children would lead to individual autonomy and emotional strength, and thus would not be consonant with the interests of those in power. However, this oppression and this forcing of submission do not only begin in the office, factory or political party;

they begin in the very first weeks of an infant's life. Afterwards they are internalized and repressed and are then, because of their very nature, inaccessible to argument. Nothing is changed in the character of submission or dependency, when it is only their object that is changed.

Therapeutic effects (in the form of temporary improvement) may be achieved if a strict superego can be replaced by the analyst's more tolerant one. The aim of analysis, however, is not to correct the patient's fate, but to enable him to confront both his own fate and his mourning over it. The patient has to discover the parents of his early years in the transference, and within himself, and must become consciously aware of his parents' unconscious manipulation and unintended contempt, so that he can free himself from them. So long as he has to make do with a tolerant substitute superego, borrowed from his analyst, his contemptuous introject will remain unchanged, and hidden in his unconscious, despite all his better conscious knowledge and intentions. Although this contemptuous introject will show itself in the patient's human relationships and will torment him, it will be inaccessible to any working through. The contents of the unconscious, as Freud said, remain unchanged and timeless. Change can only begin as these contents become conscious.

THE LONELINESS OF THE CONTEMPTUOUS

The contempt shown by narcissistically disturbed patients (to which Kernberg points with much emphasis, 1970) may have various forerunners in their life history. These may have been, for instance, 'the stupid little brothers and sisters', or the uneducated parents who don't understand anything—but the function all these expressions of contempt have in common is the defence against unwanted feelings. Contempt for younger siblings often hides envy of them, just as contempt for the parents often helps to ward off the pain of being unable to idealize them. Contempt also may serve as a defence against other feelings, and it will lose its point when it fails as a shield—for instance, against shame over one's unsuccessful courting of the parent of the opposite sex; or against the feeling of inadequacy in rivalry with the same-sex parent; and above all against narcissistic rage that the object is not completely available. So long as one despises the other person and overvalues one's own achievements ('he can't do what I can do'), one does not have to mourn the fact that love is not forthcoming without achievement. Nevertheless, avoiding this mourning means that one remains at bottom the one who is despised. For I have to despise everything in myself that is not wonderful, good, and clever. Thus I perpetuate intrapsychically the loneliness of childhood: I despise weakness, impotence, uncertainty—in short, the child in myself and in others.

The patient seldom directly expresses his contempt for the analyst at the beginning of treatment. At first his scorn is consciously directed at other people. He thinks, for example: 'I don't need any childish feelings, they are all right for my younger brothers and sisters, who do not have my judgement. Anyway, it is only sentimental stuff, ridiculous. I am grown up, I can think and act, I can make changes in things around me, I don't need to feel helpless any more, or dependent. If I am afraid, I can do something about it or try to understand it intellectually. My intelligence is my most reliable companion.'

Well, all that sounds pretty good. But the analysand comes to analysis because he feels lonely, despite or even because of his clear superiority, and because he suffers from difficulties in making contacts, or perhaps he comes because he suffers from compulsions or perversions. In the course of analysis it can then be seen how far this contempt has protected him from his own feelings.

Sometimes contemptuous feelings toward the analyst will show up very early in the analysis. But this can only be worked through when the analysand has found the broader basis for his whole world of feeling on which he can then play out and work through his ambivalence. It is then decisive that the analyst should not let himself be provoked into demonstrating his own superiority to the patient. The contempt that Kernberg describes as ubiquitous in grandiose, successful people always includes contempt for their own true selves. For their scorn implies: without these qualities, which I have, a person is completely worthless. That means further: without these achievements, these gifts, I could never be loved, would never have been loved. Thus the small, powerless child, who is helplessly dependent on others, and also the awkward or difficult child will have to suffer contempt. Grandiosity guarantees that the illusion continues: I was loved.

Those whose grandiose, false self needs to act out this certainty are often envied or admired by those whose narcissistic disturbance has a primarily depressive structure, whereas the grandiose will despise the depressives. Nevertheless, this is no basis for a typology, since grandiosity and depression expresses the same underlying problem.

Contempt as a rule will cease with the beginning of mourning for the irreversible that cannot be changed. For contempt, too, had in its own way served to deny the reality of the past. It is, after all, less painful to think that the others do not understand because they are too stupid. Then one can make efforts to explain things to them. This is the process, described by Kohut (1971), that takes place when idealization of the self-object fails and the grandiose self has to be cathected. There seems to be a way out, in fantasy at least. Through (one's own) grandiosity, power as such can be salvaged, and so the illusion of being understood ('if only I can express myself properly') can be maintained.* If however this effort is relaxed, one is forced to see how little there was on the other side and how much one had invested oneself (cf. pp. 105–6).

One must come to realize that here a general understanding as such is not possible, since each person

---

* Devastating examples of this process are the works of Van Gogh and of the Swiss painter Max Gubler, who so wonderfully and so unsuccessfully courted the favour of their mothers with all the means at their disposal.

is individually stamped by his own fate and his own childhood. Many parents, even with the best intentions, cannot always understand their child, since they, too, have been stamped by their experience with their own parents and have grown up in a different generation. It is indeed a great deal when parents can respect their children's feelings even when they cannot understand them. There is no contempt in saying, 'it was not possible'—it is a reconciliatory recognition that is hard to achieve. A detailed example may illustrate this.

A patient who had sought a second analysis because of tormenting obsessions repeatedly dreamed that he was on a lookout tower that stood in a swampy area, at the edge of a town dear to him. From there he had a lovely view, but he felt sad and deserted. There was an elevator in the tower, and in the dream there were all kinds of difficulties over entrance tickets and obstacles on the way to this tower. In reality, the town had no such tower, but it belonged unequivocally to the patient's dream landscape, and he knew it well. The phallic meaning of this dream had been considered in his previous analysis, and it was certainly not wrong to see this aspect, though it was obviously not sufficient, since the dream recurred later with the same feelings of being deserted. Interpretation of instinctual conflicts had absolutely no effect, the obsessional symptoms remained unchanged.

Only after much had changed in the course of analysis were there new variations in the dream, too, and at last it changed in a decisive way. The patient first was surprised to dream that he already had entrance tickets, but the tower had been demolished and there was no longer a view. Instead, he saw a bridge that joined the swampy district to the town. He could thus go on foot into the town and saw 'not everything' but 'some things close up'. The patient, who suffered from an elevator phobia, was somehow relieved, for riding in this elevator had caused him considerable anxiety. Speaking of the dream, he said he was perhaps no longer dependent on always having a complete view, on always seeing everything, being on top, and cleverer than other people. He now could go on foot like everyone else.

The patient was the more astonished when, toward the end of his analysis, he dreamed that he was suddenly sitting in this elevator in the tower again and was drawn upward as in a chair lift without feeling any fear. He enjoyed the ride, got out at the top and, strange to say, there was colourful life all about him. It was a plateau, and from it he had a view of the valleys. There was also a town up there, with a bazaar full of colourful wares; a school where children were practising ballet and he could join in (this had been a childhood wish); and groups of people holding discussions with whom he sat and talked. He felt integrated into this society, just as he was. This dream impressed him deeply and made him happy, and he said:

'My earlier dreams of the tower showed my isolation and loneliness. At home, as the eldest, I was always ahead of my siblings, my parents could not match my intelligence, and in all intellectual matters I was alone [the town he loved was a European centre of culture]. On the one hand, I had to demonstrate my

133

knowledge, in order to be taken seriously, and on the other, I had to hide it or my parents would say: "Your studies are going to your head! Do you think you are better than everyone else, just because you had the chance to study? Without your mother's sacrifice and your father's hard work you would never have been able to do it." That made me feel guilty and I tried to hide my differences, my interests, and my gifts. I wanted to be like the others. But that would have meant being untrue to myself.'

So the patient had searched for his tower and had struggled with obstacles (on the way, with entrance tickets, his fears, and more), and when he got to the top—that is, was cleverer than the others—he felt lonely and deserted.

It is a well-known and common paradox that parents take up this grudging and competitive attitude towards their child (understandable in view of their envy), and at the same time urge him on to the greatest achievement and (in identification) are proud of his success. Thus the patient *had to* look for his tower and had to encounter obstacles, too. In his analysis he went through a revolt against this pressure towards achievement, and so the tower disappeared in the first of the dreams I have described here. He could give up his grandiose fantasy of seeing *everything* from above and could look at things in his beloved town (into his self) from close to. The second dream came at a time when he first succeeded in expressing and experiencing himself in an artistic profession, and was receiving a lively echo. This time he did not meet the proud and envious parent figures whom he feared, but true partners in a group.

Thus ended not only his 'tower' existence, but almost at the same time his contempt for others who were not so clever and quick (for instance, in his first, highly specialized profession).

Only now did it become clear to him that he had felt compelled to isolate himself from others by means of his contempt and at the same time was isolated and separated from his true self (at least from its helpless, uncertain part). The integration of this side of his personality put him in the way of a daring and very successful change of profession that gave him much happiness. And now, after five years of analysis, this patient could become aware of his Oedipal fate with an intensity and richness of feeling that perhaps no one could have suspected earlier in this scornful, distant and intellectualizing man.

ACHIEVING FREEDOM FROM THE CONTEMPTUOUS INTROJECTS

Sexual perversions and obsessional neuroses are not the only possibilities of perpetuating the tragedy of early suffering from contempt. There are countless forms in which we may observe the fine nuances of this tragedy. The child in the adult is full of narcissistic rage against his mother because she was not available to him and because she rejected some parts of his self, and in the analysis, for instance, this rage at first finds expression in the same form as that in which he felt rejected by his mother.

There are many ways in which one may transmit the

discrimination under which one has suffered as a child. There are people, for example, who never say a loud or angry word, who seem to be only good and noble, and who still give others the palpable feeling of being ridiculous or stupid or too noisy, at any rate too common compared with themselves. They do not know it and surely do not intend it, but this is what they radiate. They have introjected a parental attitude of which they have never been aware. The children of such parents find it particularly difficult to formulate any reproach in their analysis.

Then there are the people who can be very friendly, perhaps a shade patronizing, but in whose presence one feels as if one were nothing. They convey the feeling that they are the only ones who exist, the only ones who have anything interesting or relevant to say. The others can only stand there and admire them in fascination, or turn away in disappointment and sorrow about their own lack of worth, unable to express themselves in these persons' presence. These people might be the children of grandiose parents, with whom these children had no hope of rivalry, and so later, as adults, they unconsciously pass on this atmosphere to those around them.

Now those people who, as children, were intellectually far beyond their parents and therefore admired by them, but so also had to solve their own problems alone, will give us quite a different impression. These people will give us a feeling of their intellectual strength and willpower, and they also seem to demand that we, too, ought to fight off any feeling of weakness with intellectual means. In their presence one feels one can't be recognized as a person with problems—just as they and their problems had not been recognized by their parents, for whom they always had to be strong.

Keeping these examples in mind, it is easy to see why some professors, who are quite capable of expressing themselves clearly, will use such complicated and convoluted language when they present their ideas that the students can only acquire them in a fog of anger and diligence—without being able to make much use of them. These students then may well have the same sorts of feelings that their teacher once had and was forced to suppress in relation to his parents. If the students themselves become teachers one day, they will have the opportunity of handing on this unusable knowledge, like a pearl of great price (because it had cost them so much).

It greatly aids the success of analytic work when the patient can become aware of the inner objects that work within him. Here is an example: at a certain point in her analysis a patient suddenly began to help her very intelligent ten-year-old daughter with her schoolwork, although the girl never had any difficulty in doing it alone. The patient's conscious motive was a bit of general advice from the teacher at a parent-teacher meeting. The child soon lost her spontaneity in learning, became unsure of herself, and actually began to have difficulty with her schoolwork. Now the patient's continued supervision of her daughter's homework was fully justified. The patient's own mother, a teacher, had been very proud of her pedagogic talent.

She could, as she put it, 'make something out of any child'. She was one of those unsure mothers who would even teach their children to walk and talk, if they could. By then both the patient and I knew this, for the patient had repeatedly experienced her mother in me in the transference, and she had fantasized that I was less concerned with her than with my own success and the confirmation of my own value in wanting her analysis to turn out well. Thereafter, she had remembered and experienced in her dreams scenes with her mother that confirmed these feelings. But that did not suffice. The patient also needed to discover her mother in *herself*, had to see how she had become so afraid—quite unrealistically—that her daughter would compromise her, in her ability as a mother, before the teacher. She hated her own compulsion to meddle in her daughter's life, and experienced it as something foreign to her nature, but she could not give up this need to supervise the child. At last she found help through her dreams, in which she felt that she herself was in her mother's situation during the postwar period. Now she was able to imagine how it had been for her mother, who had been widowed early and had to make her own way, for herself and her daughter, and apparently also had to contend with 'public opinion', which had it that because she went out to work she was neglecting her daughter. Her only child, my patient, had therefore to be the more perfect. The family constellation in the daughter's case was quite different, however, and the need to supervise her child disappeared when my patient realized this difference. 'I am a different person and my fate is different from that of my mother,' she once said. As a result, not only the teacher, but also her husband and neighbours 'spontaneously' stopped giving her 'good advice', and veiled orders.

There are moments in every analysis when dammed-up demands, fears, criticism, or envy break through for the first time. With amazing regularity these impulses appear in a guise that the patient has never expected or that he might even have rejected and feared all his life (cf. pp. 33–4). Before he can develop his own form of criticism he first adopts his father's hated vocabulary or nagging manner. And the long repressed anxiety will surface in—of all things!—his mother's irritating hypochondriacal fears. It is as if the 'badness' in the parents that had caused a person the most suffering in his childhood and that he had always wanted to shun, has to be discovered within himself, so that reconciliation will become possible. Perhaps this also is part of the never-ending work of mourning that this personal stamp must be accepted as part of one's own fate before one can become at least partially free.

When the patient has truly emotionally worked through the history of his childhood and thus regained his sense of being alive—then the goal of the analysis has been reached. Afterwards, it is up to the patient whether he will take a regular job or not; whether he wants to live alone or with a partner; whether he wants to join a political party, and if so, which one—all that is his own decision. His life story, his experiences, and what he has learned from them will all play a role in how he will live. It is not the task of the analyst to 'socialize' him, or 'to bring him up' (not even politically, for every form of bringing-up denies his autonomy), nor to make 'friendships possible for him'—all that is his own affair.

When the patient, in the course of his analysis, has consciously repeatedly experienced (and not only learned from the analyst's interpretations) how the whole process of his bringing-up did manipulate him in his childhood, and what desires for revenge this has left him with, then he will see through manipulation quicker than before and will himself have less need to manipulate others. Such a patient will be able to join groups without again becoming helplessly dependent or bound, for he has gone through the helplessness and dependency of his childhood in the transference. He will be in less danger of idealizing people or systems if he has realized clearly enough how as a child he had taken every word uttered by mother or father for the deepest wisdom. He may experience, however, while listening to a lecture or reading a book, the same old childish fascination and admiration—but he will recognize at the same time the underlying emptiness or human tragedy that lurks behind these words and shudder at it. Such a person cannot be tricked with fascinating, incomprehensible words, since he has matured through his own experience. Finally, a person who has consciously worked through the whole tragedy of his own fate will recognize another's suffering more clearly and quickly, though the other may still have to try to hide it. He will not be scornful of others' feelings, whatever their nature, because he can take his own feelings seriously. He surely will not help to keep the vicious circle of contempt turning.

All these things are not demands I make on my patients because of my own wishes or ideology; they are simply the result of the experience that I have gained through my work with my analysands, and that can be attributed to the effects of their regained sense of being truly alive.

Appendix

'For some years now there has been proof that the devastating effects of the traumatization of children take their inevitable toll on society. This knowledge concerns every single one of us, and – if disseminated widely enough – should lead to fundamental changes in society, above all to a halt in the blind escalation of violence. The following points are intended to amplify my meaning:

1. All children are born to grow, to develop, to live, to love, and to articulate their needs and feelings for their self-protection.

2. For their development children need the respect and protection of adults who take them seriously, love them, and honestly help them to become oriented in the world.

3. When these vital needs are frustrated and children are instead abused for the sake of adults' needs by being exploited, beaten, punished, taken advantage of, manipulated, neglected, or deceived without the intervention of any witness, then their integrity will be lastingly impaired.

4. The normal reactions to such injury should be anger and pain; since children in this hurtful kind of environment, however, are forbidden to express their anger and since it would be unbearable to experience their pain all alone, they are compelled to suppress their feelings, repress all memory of the trauma, and idealize those guilty of the abuse. Later they will have **no memory of what was done to them.**

5. Disassociated from the original cause, their feelings of anger, helplessness, despair, longing, anxiety, and pain will find expression in destructive acts against others (criminal behaviour, mass murder) or against themselves (drug addiction, alcoholism, prostitution, psychic disorders, suicide).

6. If these people become parents, they will then often direct acts of revenge for their mistreatment in childhood against their own children, whom they use as scapegoats. Child abuse is still sanctioned – indeed, held in high regard – in our society as long as it is defined as child-rearing. It is a tragic fact that parents beat their children in order to escape the emotions stemming from how they were treated by their own parents.

7.   If mistreated children are not to become criminals or mentally ill, it is essential that **at least once in their life** they come in contact with a person who knows without any doubt that the environment, not the helpless, battered child, is at fault. In this regard, knowledge or ignorance on the part of society can be instrumental in either saving or destroying a life. Here lies the great opportunity for relatives, social workers, therapists, teachers, doctors, psychiatrists, officials, and nurses **to support the child and to believe her or him**.

8.   Till now, society has protected the adult and blamed the victim. It has been abetted in its blindness by theories, still in keeping with the pedagogical principles of our great-grandparents, according to which children are viewed as crafty creatures, dominated by wicked drives, who invent stories and attack their innocent parents or desire them sexually. In reality, children tend to blame themselves for their parents' cruelty and to absolve the parents, whom they invariably love, of all responsibility.

9.   For some years now, it has been possible to prove, thanks to the use of new therapeutic methods, that repressed traumatic experiences in childhood are stored up in the body and, although remaining unconscious, exert their influence even in adulthood. In addition, electronic testing of the foetus has revealed a fact previously unknown to most adults: **a child responds to and learns both tenderness and cruelty from the very beginning**.

Appendix

10. In the light of this new knowledge, even the most absurd behaviour reveals its formerly hidden logic once the traumatic experiences of childhood no longer must remain shrouded in darkness.

11. Our sensitization to the cruelty with which children are treated, until now commonly denied, and to the consequences of such treatment will as a matter of course bring to an end the perpetuation of violence from generation to generation.

12. People whose integrity has not been damaged in childhood, who were protected, respected, and treated with honesty by their parents, will be – both in their youth and adulthood – intelligent, responsive, empathic, and highly sensitive. They will take pleasure in life and will not feel any need to kill or even hurt others or themselves. They will use their power to defend themselves but not to attack others. They will not be able to do otherwise than to respect and protect those weaker than themselves, including their children, because this is what they have learned from their own experience and because it is **this** knowledge (and not the experience of cruelty) that has been stored up inside them from the beginning. Such people will be incapable of understanding why earlier generations had to build up a gigantic war industry in order to feel at ease and safe in this world. Since it will not have to be their unconscious life-task to ward off intimidation experienced at a very early age, they will be able to deal with attempts at intimidation in their adult life more rationally and more creatively.'

References

Abraham, K. 1960 (orig. 1912). Notes on psychoanalytic investigations and treatment of manic-depressive insanity and allied conditions in *Selected papers on psychoanalysis*. New York: Basic Books, pp. 137–56.

Chasseguet-Smirgel, J. 1973. *L'ideal du moi* XIII⁰ Congrès des Psychanalystes de Langues romanes, R.P.F. 5 June 1973.

Eicke-Spengler, M. 1977. Zur Entwicklung der Theorie der Depression. *Psyche* 31:1077–125.

Fischer, R. 1976. Die psychoanalytische Theorie der Depression. *Psyche* 30:924–6.

Freud, S. (orig. 1914). Recollection, repetition, and working through. Standard Edition 12. London: Hogarth Press.

———. 1957 (orig. 1917). Mourning and melancholia. Standard Edition 14. London: Hogarth Press.

Ganz, H. 1966. *Pestalozzi*. Zurich: Origo.

Habermas, J. 1970. Der universalitätsanspruch der Hermeneutik. In *Kultur und Kritik*. Frankfurt: Suhrkamp.

Hesse, H. 1965. *Demian*. New York: Harper & Row.

———. 1970. *Gesammelte Werke*. Frankfurt: Suhrkamp.

———. 1966. Kindheit und Jugend vor Neunzehnhundert.

References

Herman Hesse in *Briefen und Lebenszeugnissen 1877–1895*. Frankfurt: Suhrkamp.

——. 1971. A Child's Heart. In *Klingsor's last summer*. New York: Farrar, Straus & Giroux.

Jacobson, E. 1971. *Depression*. New York: International Universities Press.

Joffe, W. and Sandler J. 1965a. Notes on a childhood depression. *International Journal of Psychoanalysis* 46:88–96.

——. 1965b. Notes on pain, depression, and individuation. *Psychoanalytic Study of the Child* 20:394–424.

Kernberg, O. F. 1970. Factors in the psychoanalytic treatment of narcissistic personalities. *Journal of the American Psychoanalytic Association* 18:51–85.

——. 1974. Further contributions to the narcissistic personalities. *International Journal of Psychoanalysis* 55:215, 240.

Khan, M. M. R. 1974. *The privacy of the self*. London: Hogarth Press.

Kohut, H. 1971. *The analysis of self*. New York: International Universities Press.

——. 1973. Überlegungen zum Narzissmus und zur narzisstischen Wut. *Psyche* 27:513–54.

Lavater-Sloman, M. 1977. *Pestalozzi*. Zurich and Munich: Artemis.

Levin, S. 1965. Some suggestions for treating the depressed patient. *Psychoanalytic Quarterly* 34:37–65.

Mahler, M. 1968. *On human symbiosis and the vicissitudes of individuation*. New York: International Universities Press.

Miller, A. 1971. Zur Behandlungstechnik bei sogenannten narzisstischen Neurosen. *Psyche* 25:641–68.

——. 1979. Depression and grandiosity as related forms of narcissistic disturbances. *International Review of Psychoanalysis* 6:61, 76.

——. 1979. The drama of the gifted child and the

References

psychoanalysts narcissistic disturbance. *International Journal of Psychoanalysis* 60:47, 58.

———. 1980. *Am Anfang war Erziehung*. Frankfurt: Suhrkamp. 1983. *For Your Own Good*. New York: Farrar, Straus and Giroux and London: Faber and Faber.

———. 1981. *Du sollst nicht merken*. Frankfurt: Suhrkamp.

Müller-Braunschweig, H. 1974. Psychopathologie und Kreativität. *Psyche* 28:600–654.

Nagera, H. 1967. *Vincent van Gogh*. London: Allen and Unwin.

Robertson, J. 1975. Neue Beobachtungen zum Trennungsverhalten kleiner Kinder. *Psyche* 29:626–64.

Schafer, R. 1972. Die psychoanalytische Anschauung der Realität. *Psyche* 26:882–98 and 952–71.

Spitz, R. 1967. Vom Säugling zum Kleinkind. Stuttgart: Klett.

Stern, M. M. 1972. Trauma, Todesangst und Furcht vor dem Tod. *Psyche* 26:901–26.

Winnicott, D. W. 1956. Primary maternal preoccupation. In *Collected papers*. New York: Basic Books, pp. 303–5.

———. 1960. The theory of parent-infant relationship. *International Journal of Psychoanalysis* 41:585–95.

———. 1965. *Maturational processes and the facilitating environment: Studies in the theory of emotional development*. New York: International Universities Press.

———. 1964. *The child, the family, and the outside world*. New York: Penguin.

———. 1969. The use of an object. *International Journal of Psychoanalysis* 50:700, 716.

———. 1971. *Playing and reality*. New York: Basic Books.

———. 1971. *Therapeutic consultations in child psychiatry*. New York: Basic Books.

Index

abandonment, 25–7, 103, 113
Abraham, Karl, on depression, 83
achievement, 20, 21, 56, 72
adaptation, 24, 79–82, 110
admiration, 58, 59, 60
adolescence, *see* puberty
ageing, 60–1
aggression, 50, 64, 83
alcohol, 98
alienation, from self, 20, 47, 70
ambivalence, 34–5, 51, 130
analysand, 19–21, 39–40, 74–7; relation with analyst, 99–101, 111–13, 115–16, 129–30; wish for a child, 102–4, 105; *see also* analysis; countertransference; transference
analysis, 17–18, 32–6, 75–9, 129–35, 140; autonomy and, 39–40; breakthrough in, 74, 139; and depression, 69–74; discovery and acceptance in, 17–18; experiencing in, 100, 140; and memories, 126–7; and mirroring, 69; of mother, 52–3; and obsessional neurosis, 111–14; pain in, 19–20, 26, 30, 74; and repression, 22, 107; *see also* mourning; transference; true self, discovery of
analyst, 32, 33, 38, 76–8, 105, 115; analysis of, 37–9; narcissism in, 23, 37–40; patient relation with, 99–101, 111–13, 115–16, 129–30; *see also* analysis; countertransference; manipulation
anger, 24, 100, 126

Index

anxiety, 20, 24, 105
artists, childhood, 18–19
authoritarianism, 23
autobiography, 18
autonomy, 21, 39–40, 51, 79

Balzac, Honoré de, *Le Lys dans la vallée*, 55
Beckett, Samuel, 62
Bergman, Ingmar, 93–5
biography, 18
bond permanence, 28

cathexis, 48, 49, 55, 76, 131
Chestnut Lodge field study, 57–8
child, 97–8; and cathexis, 55; and contempt, 85–94, 98; idealization of mother-love, 18–19; and introjection, 108, 109; loneliness and desertion, 19–21, 24–9; manipulation of, 44–5; need for respect, 21; patient's wish for one, 102–4, 105; and seduction, 96–8; suppression of feelings of, 73–4, 126; *see also* narcissism, healthy
compulsion to repeat, 42, 105–7; and grandiosity, 57, analysis, 33; and contempt, 88; examples of, 102–3, 105–7; and gradiosity, 57, 59; negative side of, 101, 111; and partner choice,

104, 106; and perversion, 109–11; positive side of, 101–2
conformity, 64
confusion, 69
contempt, 85–94, 109–14, 128–35
countertransference, 100–1, 113
creativity, 127
cruelty, 91, 95

Daudet, Alphonse, *Lettres de mon moulin*, 45–6
death instinct, 101
defence mechanisms, 27, 55, 59, 73, 92–4, 99; contempt as, 88–9, 90, 128–35; theory and, 116
denial, 64, 84, 127, 131; as defence mechanism, 26–7, 92; and depression, 37, 70–1; and guilt, 109; identification of, 32; of true self, 37, 80–2
depravity, 118–22
depression, 14, 69–74, 77–9, 83–4; aetiology of, 57; and childhood loneliness, 19–20; and denial, 37, 70–1; the gifted and, 19–20, 57; and grandiosity, 20, 56–7, 60–4, 76–7, 130–1; and loss of self, 47, 64–5; and society, 79–82; and true self, 80
despair, 77

discrimination, 112, 136–7
disgust, 77
displacement, 59, 92
drive theory, 15, 21
drugs, 98

ego, *see* self; true self; false self
egoism, 12–14
Eicke-Spengler, M., 58
emotional development, 55
emotional needs, 30, 49, 53, 57
empathy, 20, 98
envy, 24, 58–9, 64, 69, 77, 129

false self, 14–15, 27, 28, 29, 68–9; and analysis, 77, 78; in children, 45; in depression and grandiosity, 61, 64
fear, 88, 104
feelings, experience of, 24–5
Fellini, Federico, 60
Fischer, R., 78
Freud, Sigmund, 12, 18, 29–30, 83, 96, 126, 128; 'Mourning and Melancholy', 83; 'Recollection, Repetition and Working Through', 25

Ganz, H., 43 and n.
gifted child, 19–20, 122–3
grandiosity, 37, 56–60, 68, 130–1; as defence mechanism, 109; and depression, 20, 56–7, 60–4, 76–7, 130–1; examples of, 131n.; fantasies of, 31–2
gratification, 22, 58
greed, 77
Gubler, Max, 131n.
guilt, 20, 64, 109

Habermas, Jurgen, 25, 27
Hamburg, 113–14
Hesse, Hermann, 85, 108–9, 117–25; 'A Child's Heart' ('Kinderseele'), 119n., 122, 124; *Demian*, 118–20, 121, 124; *Hermann Lauscher*, 124
Hesse, Johannes, 123–4
Hesse, Marie, 108, 123, 124
Hitler, Adolf, 95
humiliation, 85–94, 98, 114

idealization, 18, 92, 95, 108–9, 126, 129, 131
illusion, 17, 78, 127
image formation, 120–1
impotence, 24, 69
individuation, 21, 28, 53
indoctrination, 97
instinct, 15–16, 89, 96, 113, 118, 119
introject, 29, 72, 126, 135–40; and analysis, 34, 128; loss of self and, 64
introjection, 27, 41, 108, 109, 114, 118, 119
introspection, 20

Jacobson, Edith, on depression, 84
jealousy, 24, 34, 69, 77, 113
Joffe, W., on depression, 83

Kernberg, Otto, 58–9, 128–9, 130
Khan, Masud, 40n.
Kleist, Heinrich von, *Käthchen von Heilbronn*, 29
Kohut, Heinz, 21, 47–8, 131

Lavater-Sloman, M., 43
Levin, S., 78
loneliness, 24, 113; childhood, 19–21, 24–9
love of self, 14; *see also* narcissism

Mahler, Margaret, 21, 47, 49, 52
manic-depressive psychosis, 57–8, 61
manipulation, 40–2, 44, 78, 100, 140
menopause, 56
metapsychology, 95–6, 116–17
Miller, A., 22, 65
mirroring, 31, 49, 52, 61
Moore, Henry, and mother-love, 18
moral masochism, 63
mother, 22–3 and n., 48, 49–55, 65–8; and compulsion to repeat, 44–5; contempt of, 125; idealization of, 18, 90, 126; instinct of, 65–8; and interaction with child, 49, 107–8; and introjection, 41; manipulation of child, 44–5; narcissistic needs, 51–3; narcissistically deprived, 22, 24, 25–6; as object, 104; rejection by, 112, 135; respect, 13–14; and separation, 21; and socialization of the child, 13, 125–8; *see also* parents
mourning, 36, 69, 73, 113, 129, 131, 139; in analysis, 30, 31, 37, 44, 76, 79, 127; in recovery, 62, 77, 109
'Mourning and Melancholy' (Freud), 83
Müller-Braunschweig, H., 62n.

Nagera, H., 55
narcissism, 11–16; healthy, 15, 21, 38, 49–51, 83–4
narcissistic cathexis, 23, 29, 35, 48, 57, 64, 76; and the child, 49, 55, 96
narcissistic disturbance, 24–9, 51–6, 57–8, 60–1, 63, 69–72; and childhood loneliness, 19–21, 24–9; examples of, 40–3, 53–5, 108–9, 118–20; and insight, 30; and needs of patient, 107–11; in partially adapted

Index

child, 80–1; and politics, 127; and self-object, 83–4; siblings, 55; treatment of, 15–16, 37–40; *see also* analysis; grandiosity; mother; mourning, in recovery

narcissistic needs, 24, 51–2, 127

narcissistic rage, 48, 135

Narcissus, legend of, 68–9

Nazism, 95

object-loss, fear of, 104

object-love, 14, 51, 59–60, 69

object relation, 48, 98

obsessional neurosis, 41, 90, 109–14, 135

Oedipal conflict, 26, 31, 39, 59, 89, 102, 113

oversensitivity, 64

Ovid, 68

parents, 96, 109, 118; and child, 40–2, 43, 44–5, 88–91, 106–7, 122–3, 132, 134; and child's egoism, 12–13; and childhood loneliness, 19–20, 24–9; compulsion of, 22, 117; and contempt, 12–13, 85–94, 129; needs of, 22–3; and prohibitions, 120–1; *see also* mother

patient, *see* analysand

perfectionism, 64

perversion, 32, 35, 41, 42, 90, 109–14, 135

Pestalozzi, Heinrich, 43

phallic narcissism, 59–60, 61

primary objects, 71, 114

psychosomatic symptoms, 73

puberty, 74, 80, 118; and emotional changes, 45

rage, 77, 113; *see also* narcissistic rage

reaction formation, 29

reality, 96, 127

'Recollection, Repetition and Working Through' (Freud), 25

reconciliation, 139

repression, 16, 27, 63, 95, 98; of needs and emotions, 22, 53, 74, 107

respect, 13–14, 21, 24, 26, 31

restlessness, 64

Robertson, J., 47

Rousseau, Jean Jacques, 43

St Pauli, 113–14

Sandler, J., on depression, 83

Schafer, Roy, 41n.

self, 19–20, 21, 22; loss of, 14–15, 47, 64–5, 83; *see also* false self; true self

self-alienation, 20, 47, 70

self-confidence, 65

self-esteem, 21, 50, 57, 64

self-expression, 105–7

self-love, 14; *see also* narcissism

separation, 21, 29, 37, 51

sexual seduction, 96–7

Shakespeare, William, 29–30

shame, 20, 64, 69, 88, 105, 106

siblings, 19, 23, 55, 94, 129–30; jealousy, 24

social isolation, 58

Spitz, R., 47

splitting off, 31, 42, 43, 44, 52, 63, 88–9, 110

Stern, 113–14

Stern, M., 40n.

Stravinsky, Igor, 62n.

suicide, 78–9

toilet-training, 19, 54

transference, 33–5, 100–1, 109–10, 112–13

trauma, re-enactment of, 101

true self, discovery of, 27, 28–37, 77–8, 99; disorder of, 41–2, 80–1, 101, 111, 130–1; drive theory, 15; and healthy narcissism, 15; loss of, 14–15; and mirroring, 69

truth, 17

unconscious, *see* introject, introjection

unconscious manipulation, 40, 44

Van Gogh, Vincent, 55, 131n.

Winnicott, D. W., 16, 21, 27, 32, 36, 37, 47, 49, 71, 73, 84, 116